EP

1: EW

7 NOV 20

N 2,

Toy Theatres

OF THE WORLD

★ ★ ★ ★ ★ ★ ★ ★ ★ ★ ★ ★ ★ ★ ★ ★ ★ ★ ★

Toy Theatres

OF THE WORLD

Peter Baldwin

★ ★

Foreword by George Speaight

★ ★

ZWEMMER

Frontispiece: The Critic

First published in 1992 by
A. Zwemmer Ltd
26 Litchfield Street
London WC2H 9NJ

ISBN 0 302 00614 1

LC 92 082836

Designed by Mavis Henley

Colour photography by Richard Goulding

Typeset, printed and bound in Great Britain
by Jolly & Barber Ltd, Rugby

In memory of Sarah

Contents

★ ★ ★ ★ ★ ★ ★ ★ ★ ★ ★ ★ ★ ★ ★ ★ ★ ★

Acknowledgements

★ ★

I wish to thank the following for their help, generosity and knowledge, without which this book may not have been written: Frank Bradley; Marguerite Fawdry of Pollock's Toy Museum; Dodie Masterman; Hildegarde Metzsch of M. and N. Reprise, Hamburg; Hanne Nelander of Prior's Dukketeater, Copenhagen; Kurt Pfluger; Herbert Zwiauer; and especially George Speaight, who allowed me access to papers and letters in his collection.

Thanks are also due to Janette Green for her tireless work on the middle stages of editing the manuscript; and to all at Philip Wilson Publishers, in particular to Daniel Giles for his indefatigable work in fine-editing my sometimes rambling text and over-laden picture collection.

Foreword

The toy theatre – whether known as the Juvenile Drama in England, the Papiertheater in German-speaking countries, Dukketeater in Denmark, Imagerie d'Epinal in France, or by whatever other name – was for generations of children a plaything of enchantment which inspired and created a unique form of art. For a handful of adult collectors it has been a quarry to be searched for in junk shops, in the folders of printsellers and in the basements of antique dealers, few of whom fully understood what it was they were selling. The intended and destined end of a toy theatre play was to be pasted on cardboard, cut out with scissors, performed upon its little stage, and finally thrown away with broken toys from the nursery. It is surprising that any examples have survived. Enough, however, have somehow escaped destruction for us to be able today to appreciate the charm of these little stages and the plays designed for them, and to recognize the important record of the nineteenth-century theatre that they embody.

I played with a toy theatre as a child, and have been fascinated by them ever since. I have continued to perform plays on them, and have found that – though the audience must be tiny – such a performance can provide a pleasant focus for a party in one's home. And I have even tried to write a history of them. But at that time I knew little or nothing of the toy theatre tradition in countries outside Britain. In recent years I have had the pleasure of meeting many enthusiasts from other countries of Europe, mostly in Denmark and Germany, and I have learnt to appreciate the chief European traditions of this genre. Hitherto there has been no book in the English language which covers the world-wide manifestations of the toy theatre. Peter Baldwin has provided just what is needed to enable us to recognize the various European schools of toy theatre design and manufacture.

The toy theatre is, indeed, important for many reasons. It was a creative domestic occupation in the family circle before children were lured to imbibe entertainment at second-hand in front of a television screen. It created a form of children's publishing that produced objects, sometimes of remarkable beauty and sometimes of charming naïvety. Above all, it has left records of productions in the human theatre that otherwise would have vanished unrecorded into the limbo of the past. For these, and many other reasons, we should ensure that the survivors of this plaything are understood, recognized, preserved and valued. I hope that Peter Baldwin's book will help to create a wider appreciation of this hitherto barely recognized little art.

GEORGE SPEAIGHT

Introduction

We should treat all the trivial things of life very seriously.
Oscar Wilde

I will go so far as to suggest that it is these things – trifling
things – that the world today stands most in need of, and that
the weighty ones are absorbing all our strength. . . . might it
not be wiser and much more sociable to concern ourselves
with trifles for a few decades . . . I have seen in most lands
that I have visited, even the miniature theatre held by grown
men . . . to be . . . of great value.
Edward Gordon Craig 1932

In any country and by whatever name they are known,
miniature theatres have fascinated men, women and children
for over 180 years. Yet the toy theatre (Juvenile Drama) is
much more than just a toy. First, it is an important reflection
on the social life of the middle-classes during the last century,
in days when children were obliged to amuse themselves. It
occupied long hours of pleasure and concentration in cutting
out, pasting and preparing a play for performance at home.

Of greater importance, perhaps, is its relation to
contemporary theatre, as it represents in miniature a broad
spectrum of the live stage. In London during the first half of
the nineteenth century, the theatre was dominated by
melodrama, romance and pantomime, all mounted in a
powerfully visual manner. Due to the absence of photography
and the limited availability of pictorial material, the spirit of
early nineteenth-century theatre can only be recaptured by
the scene and character sheets of the English Juvenile Drama.
It is difficult to judge how many of these were direct copies of
stage performances, although available evidence would

suggest that the output of toy theatre publishers between 1820 and 1850 was based almost entirely on the live theatre.

Peter Winn of the University of Victoria, British Columbia, in his comprehensive thesis on the plays of I.K.Green, has provided ample evidence to show that many of the fifty-five plays published by Green in London during the mid-nineteenth century, were adapted from successful plays currently running in the theatre.[1] In her study of a *Sadler's Wells Scene Book*,[2] Sybil Rosenfeld compared water-colour sketches of set designs by Luke Clint and John Henderson Grieve with their toy theatre counterparts. The similarities were strong enough to establish that the original sketch designs were copied for the toy theatre.

The catalogue of an exhibition of the work of Clarkson Stanfield RA (1793-1867),[3] states that although much of Stanfield's stage designs have disappeared, there is a certain amount of secondary material to indicate their appearance. The toy theatre plays an important part here. An act drop painted by Stanfield in 1823 for Drury Lane Theatre was reproduced in miniature by Hodgson and Co. That same year set designs for *The Cataract of the Ganges* (1823) were used again by Hodgson for a toy theatre play. On the Continent the opera was a common source of miniature theatre design, some of the most popular being Mozart's *The Magic Flute* and Wagner's *Ring Cycle*, reproduced by Joseph Scholz of Mainz. Stage plays were also used, particularly in Copenhagen, where the Casino Theatre provided material for the Dukketeater (toy theatre), and in the large German and Austrian cities, where stage designers were co-opted to recreate their sets on a small scale.

It was A. E. Wilson, drama critic of *The Star*, who in 1932 wrote the first history of toy theatre. His *Penny Plain, Twopence Coloured* was a well-illustrated essay drawing on examples of character prints and scene sheets. This was followed by George Speaight's *Juvenile Drama. The history of the English Toy Theatre* (1946).[4] However, both of these works confined their studies to England, ignoring the wealth of publishers in Europe and America. In describing the large number of publishers involved in promoting toy theatre, and illustrating the variety and vitality of stages, proscenia, scenery and character prints produced all over Europe, we must also be grateful to those who have accumulated substantial collections, some of which are readily accessible for research in public museums.

The Ralph Thomas Collection contained in the Print Room of the British Museum concentrates on the earlier publishers: William West, Mrs J. H. Jameson and Bernard and William Hodgson. However, inspite of this it contains only two proscenium sheets (Figs 7 and 12). Similarly, the Theatre Museum, Covent Garden, which holds the Stone and Hinkins collections, has remarkably few examples of stage fronts. Frank Bradley, whose collection is now in the Derby Museum, has balanced the situation having gathered together a remarkable array of models and sheets from around the world. Many of the illustrations in this survey are from this collection. Pollock's Toy Museum in London possesses a varied collection of early English and European theatres and a good collection of sheets.

Other fine collections in Britain include that which is now housed in the library of Christchurch College Oxford, the gift of Frank Brady, a former undergraduate, and the Museum of London's extensive Jonathan King Collection. King, who ran a newsagents in Islington, made a point of keeping an example of every Christmas card, Valentine card and Juvenile Drama sheet he sold, thereby accumulating a massive collection of items. The Puppentheatersammlung at the Stadt Museum in Munich contains a large cross-section of sheets by most of the European publishers. One of the largest private collections in Europe is held by M. and N. Reprise in Hamburg, who have been reproducing sheets from the firm of Joseph Scholz for the last twenty years. However, the presence of collections should not obscure the fact that the toy theatre was a popular children's pastime. The whole point of such things was to *perform* plays in miniature; to move small cut-out figures about the stage; to bring up good fairies or bad ghosts through sliding trapdoors; to create sound effects with whistles, coconut shells and indoor fireworks and to persuade family and household servants to watch the performance.

That a great deal of preparation was needed prior to a performance is attested in an 1871 article written by J. Oxenford, drama critic of *The Times*:

One of the great advantages pertaining to the Toy Theatre was the quantity of time that it occupied. The boy with his bare stage yet unprovided with proscenium and curtains, with his sheets and scenery yet uncoloured, was supplied with ample employment for all the spare hours of the winter holiday. . . . The actual performance was not a very brilliant affair. Yawns were frequent among the audience long before the descent of the curtain.

Despite Oxenford's reservations, performances still take place today. The Toy Theatre Society of Denmark is prolific in its productions; festivals of Paper Theatre in Germany draw performers from all over Europe. Ab Vissers from Holland is a popular player, as is George Speaight who regularly travels throughout Europe with his production of *The Miller and His Men* (Fig 1). My own theatre has featured at festivals in Denmark, Belgium, Germany and France, where I happily perform my favourite play, *The Corsican Brothers*.

It comes as no surprise to find that a whole host of actors has been drawn to the wonders of the toy theatre. Henry Irving's leading lady, Ellen Terry, wrote in *The Mask* in 1912: 'I remember the little Toy Theatres well and there is nothing quite like them. I had one when I was a child and they were known as Redington's theatres'.[5]

Terry's first stage performance is immortalized on a Matthias Trentsensky character sheet adapted from Charles Kean's production of *The Winter's Tale* at the Princesses Theatre. Her son, Edward Gordon Craig, the founder of *The Mask* magazine and an actor in Irving's company, wrote many articles on the pleasures of Juvenile Drama: 'In England we possess the best of Toy Theatres and the worst of grown up ones. We consider Pollock's Theatre as the very best . . . in the world, and that Beerbohm Tree's Theatre is the very worst grown up theatre in the world.'[6]

For Gordon Craig, as for Ellen Terry, John Gielgud, Noel Coward and a host of other leading names of the British stage, the toy theatre was perhaps the vital springboard for their journey into the glittering world of theatre.

1 George Speaight performing
The Miller and His Men

CHAPTER ONE

THE TOY THEATRE
IN ENGLAND

2 Card model of William West's shop, 13 Exeter Street, Covent Garden

3 William West

The one and only William West

Going back to the beginning of the toy theatre story in England we must look into the window of an elegant Regency shop, number thirteen Exeter Street (Fig 2). It was owned by William West, the earliest and most prolific of all toy theatre publishers.

The story begins in 1811 when West was twenty-eight years old. Exeter street ran alongside the Lyceum Theatre and close to the Theatres Royal, Drury Lane and Covent Garden, all of which provided material for many of the plays adapted and miniaturized for the toy theatre.

Many years later West described his work to Henry Mayhew in an article in the *Morning Chronicle* of 25 February 1850: 'I am a maker of children's theatres, and a theatrical print publisher. I have been in the line since 1811'. Having taken over the shop from his mother, a haberdasher, he continued to run it as a haberdashery and to run a small circulating library. In a corner of the shop stood a glass case containing a few toys and children's halfpenny lottery prints: 'The lottery things was so bad and sold so well, that the idea struck me that something theatrical would sell.' West had connections in the theatre: his father was an under property man at Covent Garden, where his sister was also a dancer: 'I took it in my head to have a print done of Mother Goose'. The print consisted of eight characters – each in a separate compartment – from a very popular pantomime playing at Covent Garden. Under the figures ran a line of foolish rhyme:

The Golden Egg and Mother Goose
Prime bang-up and no abuse
Harlequin as feather light,
And Zany's antics to please you with delight
Here's Mr Punch you plainly see
And Joan his wife both full of glee
In woman's habits does Harlequin
Deceive the clown, by name Joe Grim [1]

The enormous popularity of *Mother Goose* – it had three runs
between 1806 and 1811 – led West to publish his sheet of
characters, and thereafter artists were sent to pantomimes and
melodramas to sketch costumes and scenery for the engraver to
work up on copper plates.

Thus began the Juvenile Drama:

At first, you see, we didn't do any but the principal characters in a
piece . . . after that we was asked by the customers for theaytres
[sic] to put the characters in . . . I was obliged to keep three
carpenters to make 'em for me. I turned out the first toy theaytre
. . . in 1813. I used to make . . . about fifty toy theaytres a week. . . .
They was fitted up with very handsome fronts . . . and they had
machinery to move the side wings on and off; lamps in front, to rise
and fall with machines, and side lamps to turn on and off to darken
the stage . . . and cut traps to open for the scenery to go up and
down through the stage.

THE DESIGNS

West used the machinery of the real theatre to create his magical
world. The picture frame for this world can be seen in a large and
splendid theatre preserved in Pollock's Toy Museum in London
(Fig 4). West sold stage fronts of Drury Lane and showed Mayhew a
copy 'done by a real architectural designer [who] I got the liberty to
go and make a drawing of the front as soon as it was up after the
fire.' Drury Lane was rebuilt by J. Wyatt between 1811 and 1812
following a fire which completely burnt out the old building.
Although not a copy, this model is inspired by Wyatt's design.

4 William West,
toy theatre, *c*1820.
The scene is from *The
Maid and the Magpie*

Various additional features could be applied to the basic stage to complete the overall design. Sheets printed by West show a selection of motifs such as this stage box, as well as proscenium doors, columns and angelic figures, all of which could be adapted as the maker wished (Fig 5).

Pollock's Toy Museum also holds another theatre attributed to West (Fig 6). Approximately the same size, it too is an amalgam of various pieces. But here we also come across designs that reappear in the work of later publishers. The lower section, including the Corinthian columns and recessed arch are original West designs, as are the decorative panels, the coat of arms and the stage boxes. Examination of the top, however, reveals not only a second coat of arms, but a central panel containing putti cavorting in chariots, both of which are repeated on a proscenium supposedly by the

5 William West, detail of a stage box for use with the *New Large Stage Front*, c1820

6 William West, toy theatre, c1820. The scene is from *Harlequin Jack and the Beanstalk*.

publisher M. Skelt (*c*1840).[2] The same designs appear in reverse on a later proscenium by the publisher A. Park.[3] The top right-hand corner of the proscenium reveals further elements from other publishers' work. Thus, the demon figure supporting a vase is seen again in M. Skelt's *Harlequin Old Dame Trot* (scene 5).[4] The helmeted figure is prominent on a wing-piece in Skelt's *Wood Daemon* and below him the circular shield with the thistle in the centre is that held by Rhoderick Dhu in a later portrait of him by M. and B. Skelt (*c*1845).[5] It is possible that the the later Skelt designs were pirated from a sheet of West's; but it is most likely this model was made up sometime in the middle of the nineteenth century, the builder making use of the various designs to hand.

No trace has been found of West's copper plates: rumour has it that, having no family to inherit his business, they were broken up. However, West set the standard for future publishers; the quality of drawing, engraving and colouring of many of his surviving characters, scenes and stage fronts is exceptionally fine. Without him we might never have experienced the delights of toy theatre nor have acquired such an accurate visual knowledge of the early nineteenth-century London stage.

I. K. Green

The beginnings of the toy theatre business are so shrouded in mystery that it is impossible to give an accurate account of the early years. Nowhere is this more the case than with the publisher I. K. Green.

On 1 January 1812 the first recorded stage front to be published by I. K. Green appeared in the window of a theatrical print shop in St Martin's Lane run by H. Burtenshaw, not far from Exeter Street (Fig 7).

7 I. K. Green, stage front,
published 'as the Act directs'
1 January 1812

Published as the
Act directs, Jan.r
1.st 1811, by
I.K.GREEN.

ENCOURAGEMENT · AU · FACER · ENGESTIEX · FUSE · OVERHAO · EGENG

Published as the Act directs, Jan.r 1811, by

I.K.GREEN,
and Sold by
H.BURTENSHAW,
at his Theatrical, Military, Historical,
and COMIC Print SHOP,
N.o 130,
S.t Martins Lane,
LONDON.

INDUSTRIE

PROSPERER

MOUT

William West had an apprentice working for him by the name of Green and there has been considerable discussion by both George Speaight and A. E. Wilson about Green's pirating of West's designs.[6] From the available evidence it appears that Green abused his access to West's engraved copper plates to turn out sheets of characters under his own name, just prior to the same sheets being printed by his master. There are at least five known instances of this practice and we can only surmise that, as a sharp youth of twenty-one, Green clearly saw the potential in the prints. Having obtained West's copper plates he altered the name and one or two other details and issued the prints through Burtenshaw. Unfortunately as no surviving print exists of West's original 1812 stage front no comparison can be made between it and Green's, which is consequently the earliest stage front in existence. In 1814 Green disappeared for reasons which still remain a mystery. However, in 1832 he was back in London where for the next twenty-five years he published some fifty-five plays, some adapted from the contemporary stage, others copied from popular designs belonging to other publishers.

I William West, character sheet for *The Forty Thieves*, published 9 October 1824

In attempting to document the sources of Green's plays Peter Winn of Victoria University was helped by the fact that Green was one of the few publishers to date all his sheets.[7] With limited means at his disposal Winn was able to conclude that at least a third of Green's plays – some nineteen altogether – were based on productions at specific theatres, including six from performances at the *transpontine* Surrey Theatre. The other two thirds were from previously published plays. Difficulty arose with the many popular melodramas repeatedly revived by different companies at different theatres. Of *The Castle of Otranto* published by Green on 25 December 1841, Winn noted a number of contemporary productions, including one at Covent Garden the previous year.

A review in *The Times* described many tricks which are also illustrated by Green, albeit in simplified form, including the trick room scene: 'Furnished lodgings: the gradual progress made from a well furnished room to bare walls under the influence of the Harlequin's wand, to the great annoyance of the two lodgers Clown and Pantaloon. Chair after chair slips through the wall . . . fire irons find their way up the chimney'. Winn also discovered a

West's Characters in the *Forty Thieves.*

PLATE 4th — Price 1d. Plain.

Ocobrand.

Casim Baba.

LONDON. Published Octr. 9th 1824. by W. WEST.
at his Theatrical Print Warehouse No. 57. Wych. Street,
— *Strand.* —

Morgiana.

Ganem.
2nd Drefs.

III Hodgson and Company,
character sheet for *Ali Pacha*, published
2 December 1822

HODGSON'S, New Theatrical Characters in ALI PACHA.

Price 1ª Pl.

Woman of Yanina

Abs Soldier.

Mouchtar.

ncing Girl.

Zenocles 3rd dress.

Hassan.

Prnd Decr. 2.1822 by Hodgson & Cº 10, Newgate Street.

London. Pub. by W. WEBB. 146. Old St. St Lukes.

28

review in *The Times* of *Wapping Old Stairs* at the Surrey Theatre, which Green adapted and published on 1 February 1838. The information in the review on the characters and scenes exactly matches those of Green; the highlight of both is Tom's great leap from the mast-head of an Indiaman. Similar links were also established for *Harlequin and Riddle Me Riddle Me Ree*, performed for fifty-five nights at the Royal Olympic Theatre, and the production of *Belphegor the Conjuror* at the Queens Theatre.

IV W.G. Webb, scene 5 from
Harlequin Jack and the Beanstalk

Other contemporary publishers were quick to pick up the idea of Juvenile Drama from West and Green. In 1811 the first sheets appeared from Mrs J.H. Jameson's Theatrical Print Warehouse at 13 Duke Court, Bow Street, very close to West and the leading theatres.[8] Most of her publications were souvenir sheets and no stage fronts appear to have survived. Other publishers quickly followed, perhaps the most famous being Arthur Park.

★ ★

A. Park

In 1818 Arthur Park began publishing toy theatre sheets. He was an engraver, lithographer and publisher who, apart from toy theatre sheets, produced dissected puzzles, toy books, Twelfth Night characters, riddles and other children's ephemera.[9]

Park is a comparatively underrated early publisher, largely because his output was considerably less than that of his contemporaries. Writing in the latter half of the nineteenth century, H.S. Marks RA recalled his time as art critic of the *Spectator* when he had extolled the virtues of Park's characters: 'It would be as well for antiquarians to pay a visit to Leonard Street, Finsbury, at once and procure specimens of the works which may one day be regarded with curiosity if not admiration'.[10]

THE DESIGNS

One of the earliest extant examples of Park's work is a boxed theatre model in the private collection of Frank Bradley. Neither the model (Fig 8) nor the box (Fig 9) bear Park's name, but the play sheets that came with the package are of Park's version of *The Miller and His Men* and it seems certain that they went together as one product. The picture on the box lid (Fig 9) is especially interesting because it shows the interior of a real theatre rather than a model; it may be Covent Garden, where this particular play was first produced in 1813. Most unusually it depicts stall seats rather than the customary pit benches, thus dating it from the 1830s as one of the earliest illustrations of stalls in a theatre. Other pointers to Covent Garden as the source include the semi-elliptical dome above the proscenium arch, a feature of Robert Smirke's original design.

Throughout all Park's publications there is a strong sense of 'theatre' which his family successors were unable to maintain. In 1835 A. Park left for America and the business passed to Archibald Alexander Park.

8
A. Park,
toy theatre,
*c*1830

9
A. Park,
box lid design
for Fig 8

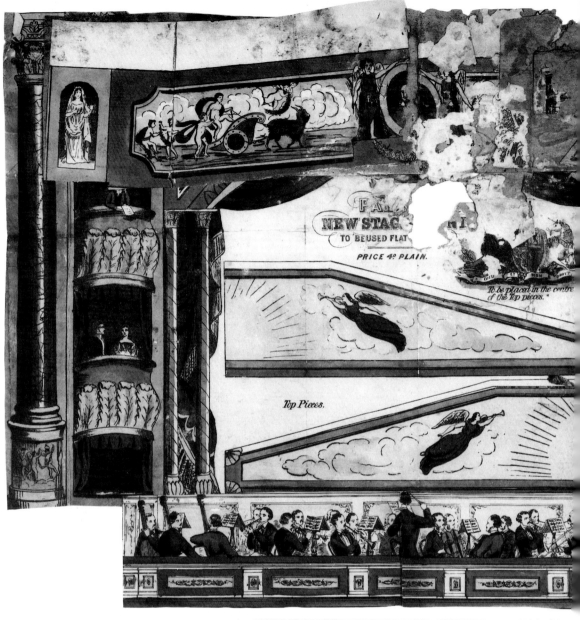

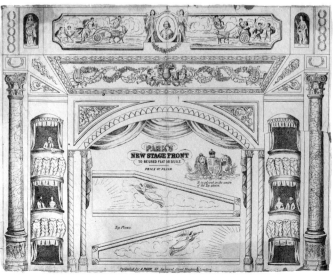

10 and 11 A. Park,
two examples of the same stage
front. Fig 10, however,
is an earlier print

An example of the deterioration in quality of the later Park publishing can be seen by comparing the details of two illustrations of the same proscenium. The first (Fig 10), a badly damaged version, is an etched hand-coloured print; the second (Fig 11) is an uncoloured lithograph. In Fig 10 the two pairs of slender 'barber's pole' Corinthian columns have the curtain extended behind them and the audience in the boxes is finely drawn. In Fig 11 the area behind the columns is left blank, without any curtain, and the audience is crudely drawn in a different hand. The same applies to the bust of Shakespeare and his supporting angels above the arch. As there is no orchestra strip accompanying Fig 11, no comparisons can be made here, except for the fact that the pit musicians in Fig 10 are very similar to those in W.G. Webb's 1870 orchestra. As W.G. Webb served his apprenticeship with Park, this may have been the former's first attempt at a design.

Comparison of these two prints points therefore to Fig 10 being the earlier version by Arthur Park. By the time Archibald decided to re-issue it, either the plate was very worn, or, he might have printed the later version from a lithographic stone, having previously transferred the design. In doing this he had to redraw parts of it directly on to the stone thus producing the result seen on the proscenium in Fig 11.

★ ★

Hodgson and Company

The Hodgsons were the first serious rivals to William West. Although there had been a Hodgson running a stationers at 11 King Street since 1799, it was not until 1820 that Bernard and William Hodgson set up a printing press at 25 Fleet Street, later extending to premises at 43 Holywell Street and finally to Newgate Street, from where the majority of their sheets were printed. They were in the toy theatre business for only eight years (1822-30). However, they managed to produce over seventy extremely well drawn and etched plays before the operation passed to Orlando Hodgson in 1831. Under O. Hodgson the drawing for the plays was almost certainly done by Robert Cruickshank, George

33

Cruickshank's elder brother. In 1986 six sheets of ink and water-colour drawings of scenes and characters for O. Hodgson's *The Giant Horse* were sold at Sotheby's. Each was signed Robert Cruickshank. 'On the grounds of style', wrote George Speaight, 'the same artist should be given credit for the rest of O. Hodgson's production'.[11]

THE DESIGNS

One of the very few stage fronts by the Hodgsons in existence is in the Ralph Thomas Collection in the British Museum (Fig 12). If Park's boxed model (cf Figs 8 and 9) was an approximation of Smirke's Covent Garden Theatre, then this earlier reproduction by Hodgson and Company is notable for its accuracy. Assuming that the dome of the real theatre was inserted in 1813 and further alterations were performed in 1819, then Hodgson would have sent his artist to the theatre sometime in the intervening years, although the actual print was not published until 1822.

★ ★

William Cole and *The British Stage in Miniature*

William Cole was a partner in Bernard and William Hodgson's firm, but continued business on his own account at 10 Newgate Street, where he appears to have sold most of the original Hodgson stock of 'scenes, characters, stage fronts, stage drops and foot pieces, with the play adapted to the same, each neatly done up in a case' (Fig 13). *The British Stage in Miniature* could be bought in one of three sizes, each plain or coloured. Thus, for nearly thirty shillings the large size, hand-coloured *Zoroaster* was the most expensive item.[12] Even an uncoloured, small version of *Maid and the Magpie* at three shillings would have taken a boy several weeks to buy. In addition, Cole advertised wooden stages, with machinery for the scenes, etc. adapted to the three sizes: first size, 6s; second size, 10s; third size, 18s. These were designed to be taken to pieces. No doubt the Hodgsons operated in much the same way, charging similar prices for high-quality products which, together with West's publications, represented some of the finest examples of toy theatre sheets and stages.

12 Hodgson and Co., *New Front of Covent Garden Theatre* published 20 September 1822.

Published by W. COLE, 10, Newgate Street.

THE
BRITISH STAGE IN MINIATURE
CONSISTING OF

Scenes, Characters, Stage Fronts, Stage Drops, and Foot Pie... with the Play adapted to the same, each neatly done up in a Ca...

	Small Size		Middle Size		Largest Si...	
	Plain s. d.	Col. s. d.	Plain s. d.	Col. s. d.	Plain s. d.	C...
Aladdin	4 6	7 9	8 9	16 0	11 9	21
Blood-Red Knight	3 6	5 9	6 6	11 0	9 10	17
Blue Beard	4 0	6 9				
Cataract of the Ganges	6 3	11 3	9 2	16 6	13 10	24
Cherry and Fair Star	5 0	8 9	9 6	17 0	13 3	24
Devil and Dr. Faustus	4 0	6 9				
Edward the Black Prince	5 10	10 6			12 9	23
Exile	5 9	10 0	8 8	15 6	11 3	20
Forty Thieves	4 3	7 3	7 6	13 0	11 3	20
Gilderoy	3 6	5 9	6 8	11 6	9 4	16
Guy Mannering	3 8	6 0	6 8	11 6	10 0	19
Hamlet	4 6	7 9	6 9	11 6	10 4	20
Life in London	5 0	10 3	9 9	17 6		
Life in Paris	4 3	7 3				
Lodoiska	3 6	5 9	6 0	10 0	8 9	18
Macbeth	4 6	8 0			12 7	23
Maid and the Magpie	3 0	4 9	5 6	9 0	8 3	15
Magna Charta	4 10	8 6	2	12 6	11 6	21
Mary, the Maid of the Inn	3 4	6 4	6 4	10 8	9 8	17
Miller and his Men	4 3	7 3	7 2	12 6	10 4	18
Montrose	4 6	7 9	7 8	13 6	12 6	23
Pizarro	3 6	5 0	6 8	11 6	9 8	17
Richard the Third	4 6	7 9	8 2	13 0	13 0	24
Rob Roy	4 2	7 0			10 11	19
Romeo and Juliet	5 0	8 9			12 9	23
Tekeli	3 6	6 0	6 3	10 6	9 0	16
Temple of Death	3 0	4 9				
Thalaba the Destroyer	4 2	7 0	7 6	13 0	11 6	24
Timour the Tartar	4 4	7 6	6 6	11 0	9 9	17
Vision of the Sun	5 9	10 3	9 8	17 6	14 5	24
Zoroaster	5 3	9 3	9 6	17 0	15 9	2

The above consist of from 20 to 60 Prints, of Scenes, Charac... &c. in each Play, according to their respective prices, and af... endless amusement, combined with rational instruction, to... youthful classes of Society. The Scenes or Characters of any p... may be had, if required, separately; with every appendage ne... sary to dramatic Action or Ornament, in a Series of splendid C... bats, Processions, and Theatrical Portraits.

N. B. *Wooden Stages*, with Machinery for the Scenes, ... adapted to the three sizes,—first size, 6s.; second size, 10s.; ... size, 18s. These are made to take to pieces, and printed direc... are given with them for their use.

Also, an entirely new and original Series of popular Dram... Pieces, entitled "THE JUVENILE DRAMA," consisting... Sixty-one separate Plays, at 6d. each, written expressly for... Scenes and characters above, and which contain no sentimer... expression improper for the tender minds of youth.

13 William Cole, *The British Stage in Miniature*, an advertisement for the Juvenile Drama

VELUTI IN SPECULUM

London Published Sep.r 20 1822 by Hodgson & Co 10. Newgate Street.

Price 2.d Pla..

★ ★

The Skelt family (1832-72)

The name of Skelt has always seemed a part and parcel of the
charm of his productions. . . . Indeed, this name of Skelt appears so
stagey and piratic, that I will adopt it boldly to design these
qualities.
Robert Louis Stevenson [13]

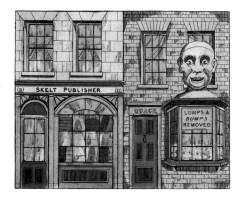

14 Skelt family, the
shop at 11 Swan Street, Minories,
from scene 11 of *Harlequin
and Old Dame Trot*

We first learn of the Skelt family in 1835 when, together with
I.K.Green, they succeeded in transforming the toy theatre into a
national pastime. This was partly the result of simple economics:
they cut the retail price of sheets and theatres by fifty per cent. In
the process the quality deteriorated; but as the sheets were there to
be cut up it seemed to matter little whether the drawing was less
artistic, the paper cheaper and the colouring stencilled.

Those members of the Skelt family involved in the toy theatre
business were listed by Ralph Thomas in an article he wrote for
Notes and Queries in 1898:

M (I believe Matthew) first started. He took another into partnership,
and their prints are published by M and M Skelt. Then one of these
Ms left and the prints again appear as published by M Skelt. This M
took a B (Benjamin I believe) into partnership and their prints are
published by M and B Skelt: then M goes out and the prints are
published by B alone, who I presume burst up like an explosion in
The Miller and His Men; but then we have some salvage from the
wreck published by E Skelt without any address. [14]

THE DESIGNS

Between them the Skelts published a number of stage fronts of
various sizes. The smallest, costing half a penny, was just
19 × 16 cm and quite impractical for performing plays.

V J.Redington, the *Neptune Theatre*
(41 × 33 cm). The scene is from the
final explosion of the mill in *The
Miller and His Men*

For a penny it was possible to purchase a more elaborate *New
Improved Stage Front* (Fig 15). Echoes of William West were included
– the angels with trumpets in the top left- and right-hand corners of

VI Benjamin Pollock Ltd,
Regency Theatre, 1946. This was
the author's first toy theatre given
to him when he was twelve years
old. Various examples of miniature
lighting can be seen behind the
curtain

15 Skelt family,
New Improved Stage Front
(penny 'shells')

the pediment being the most obvious examples (cf Fig 4). The decorous nymphs sporting themselves in clouds under the dome were slightly anachronistic, especially in view of the sea gods in their shell chariots which appeared above them. The shell motif was repeated on the lower boxes containing the audience, again in Regency costume.

16 E. Skelt *New and Improved* stage front

Coming late into the field, E. Skelt put his name – but not his address – to a much earlier design (Fig 16). It was sold for twopence plain, fourpence coloured and its grand proscenium is unusual for lacking a surmounting pediment. Ironically an identical print in the Brady Collection, published by Robert Lloyd, appears with the 'missing' pediment in place.[15]

★ ★

W.G.Webb (1820-90) and H.J.Webb (1852-1933)

William George Webb was born in Ripley, Surrey in 1820, the son of a London wool merchant. At the age of fourteen he was apprenticed for seven years 'without wages but with board, lodging and washing' to the Juvenile Drama publisher Arthur Park of Leonard Street in Finsbury, London.[16]

W.G.Webb was the only toy theatre publisher to serve an apprenticeship and consequently mastered the trade thoroughly before establishing his own business. He learnt how to draw, etch and print and as a result produced some magnificent work which, when hand-coloured, represented some of the best of the nineteenth-century Juvenile Drama sheets. Webb also wrote and adapted the plays himself and when he died in 1890 his son, H.J.Webb, continued in business as one of the last genuine toy theatre publishers until his own death in 1933.

17 W.G.Webb, shop at 49 Old Street, St Luke's, demolished in 1898, from a scene in *Harlequin, Dame Crump* (1854)

Yet the Webbs never really achieved the recognition they deserved. Much of the credit for keeping the trade alive in the first thirty years

of this century has gone to another publisher from Hoxton, London, called Benjamin Pollock (see p 52ff). This is largely the result of an essay written by Robert Louis Stevenson in 1884, which belittled Webb as 'a poor cuckoo, flaunting in Skelt's nest.... if you love Art, Folly or the bright eyes of children, speed to Pollock's.'[17] The background to this essay is slightly confused, although it would appear to centre around an encounter between Stevenson and Webb senior, in which the latter, having provided Stevenson with much background information on the subject, together with a pile of sheets for illustrations, proceeded to have an argument with the writer about his own part in the projected essay. Stevenson stormed dramatically out of the shop exclaiming, 'This is going to cost you something, Mr Webb, this is going to cost you a great deal!'

W. G. Webb is the bridge between the early and later publishers: together father and son span nearly a hundred years of toy theatre publishing. Henry James Webb was visited by most of the notable collectors and enthusiasts of the 1920s and 30s, including G. K. Chesterton, Serge Diaghilev and Winston Churchill.[18]

THE DESIGNS

The largest of the Webb theatres was the *Fourpenny Stage Front*, an example of which is in the Frank Bradley Collection in the Derby Museum (Fig 18). The orchestra was from a print by another contemporary publisher, John Redington and the scene was from his *Sleeping Beauty*.[19] The Derby stage front incorporates some unusually fanciful motifs, such as the chariots on the pediment, reminiscent of those in some of Skelt's prints (cf Figs 15 and 16). The proscenium arch is higher than usual, although it is more in keeping with the proportions of a real theatre stage of the period. In toy theatre terms it probably meant that top drops and borders were needed to hide the edges of scenes.

18 W. G. Webb, *Fourpenny Stage Front*. The scene is from *Sleeping Beauty*

The Webbs were constantly moving premises. From Cloth Fair – close to the Hodgsons – they moved to Bermondsey Street and then to a succession of addresses in Old Street, St Luke's. Pl IV has them at 146 Old Street, although it is known that they were also at numbers 49, 104 and 124. Benjamin Pollock and his father-in-law John Redington at least remained in the same shop.

★ ★

John Redington and the pilgrimage to Hoxton

The spirit of I.K. Green permeates the toy theatre world, and nowhere more so than the publishing house of John Redington – later taken over by Benjamin Pollock – at 73 Hoxton Street, London N1.[20]

Amongst the books, beads, bodkins, buttons and brushes Redington sold toy theatres (Fig 20). Having acted as retailer for I.K. Green's publications for some years, Redington later acquired his copper plates and set about re-issuing the sheets, the full list of which can be seen on the lid of his old paint box in Pollock's Toy Museum.

19 John Redington
(1819-76)

20 J. Redington,
his shop front, a
pantomime backscene
from *Harlequin
Baron Münchausen*

21 J.Redington, *New Improved Stage Front*, price halfpenny

THE DESIGNS

Redington sold a good variety of stage fronts and orchestra strips. *The Brittannia* [sic] stage came in three different sizes – at halfpenny, one penny and twopence – of which the smallest and most impractical measured only 20 × 15 cm (Fig 21). The real Britannia

45

Theatre was just down the road from Redington's shop and no doubt he used the name to attract audiences into buying souvenirs of their visits to the 5000 seat theatre. The stage front illustrated as Fig 21 is an example of the rather crude nature of Redington's smaller designs; there is a certain half-heartedness about Britannia's minions. The rather crude miniature below them would appear to be Shakespeare and the architecture is straightforward.

Redington, in common with most of the later publishers, did not date his prints. However, research by Barry Clarke of Pollock's Toy Museum has established the publication date of the *Large Theatre* proscenium (Figs 22 and 23):

Careful examination of the sheet . . . discloses the fact that the lady in the top right box is holding in her hand a playbill on which one can read the words DRURY MATHEW SEESAW. The pantomime *Seesaw Margery Daw* was performed for the first time at Drury Lane Theatre with Charles Mathews as Acting Manager on December 26th 1856 and ran well into the following year. Redington's print bears no resemblance to the Drury Lane of that date . . . but it would seem that its date of publication can be definitely determined as 1857.[21]

Thus Fig 23 was probably an original Redington publication, as he did not take Green's plates and insert his own name until the latter's death in 1860. The orchestra strip would appear to be a later print owing to the cut of the musicians' coats which are more recent than those of the gentlemen in the boxes.

Another standard and popular model, still reproduced today, was the *Neptune Theatre* (Pl V). In it Neptune rides triumphantly over the green waves, surrounded by his tritons and drawn by sea-horses, while the audience remains curiously unmoved by the activity on the stage.

22 J Redington, detail of theatre box from Fig 23

VII A. H. Mathews, *Large Stage*

X Adolf Engel, toy theatre,
c1880

23
J. Redington, the *Large Theatre*.
The scene is from *Cinderella*

★ ★

Benjamin Pollock (1856-1937)

At about this time one of the regular customers to Redington's shop was a young man by the name of Benjamin Pollock. He lived a little way to the north of Hoxton Street at 64 Albion Road. At the age of eighteen Benjamin was destined to follow his father into the fur trade. However, it was his habit to call into Redington's to buy his tobacco, and while he may have been aware of the toy theatres suspended from the ceiling, he mostly had eyes for Redington's pretty daughter, Eliza. Gradually, Benjamin became determined that Eliza should be his and on 28 May 1877, a year after Redington's death, they were married at the church of St. Michael and All Angels in the parish of South Hackney.[22]

Benjamin was at last able to abandon the fur trade in favour of a precarious living in the toy theatre business. The name on the fascia board above Redington's old shop window was changed to Pollock, where it was to remain for the next sixty-seven years.

Business was brisk. Pollock continued to print lithographic reproductions of Redington's most popular plays, colouring them in by hand during the summer when the light was better and business slacker. The only original work published by Pollock was drawn by a certain James Tofts, 'a man of substance, a draughtsman he called himself'.[23] Tofts beautifully redesigned the large scenery for *Sleeping Beauty in the Wood*, as well as a stage front with the Neptune motif again adorning the arch.

During the 1930s, following a period of decline, the shop was rediscovered by newspaper and magazine writers. Interviewed in 1930 Pollock remembered the early days: 'I had several men working for me, and it was nothing to send off half a gross of wooden stages at a time . . . a year ago or so I had to send one to Charlie Chaplin in America'.[24] Today there are still those who recall visiting the shop, some with more money than others. One of the stage hands at the original Britannia Theatre remembered using sheets he bought from Pollock's to perform plays on his own toy theatre, often to paying audiences who regularly demanded their money back at the end of the show.

24 Benjamin Pollock, the publisher in the doorway of 73 Hoxton Street, c1930

Unquestionably the shop provided glamour and adventure, but for the Pollocks it also meant a great deal of hard work in the form of printing, packaging and paperwork. Benjamin, together with his daughters Selina and Louisa, was hard pressed to meet the demands of customers. In a letter to a client dated 4 December 1936 he wrote: 'Enclosed is the best I can do. I have sent The Miller and His Men, as much coloured as in stock and the rest plain. . . . I have no top drops in stock at all and cannot promise any theatres, as I have so many orders in hand.'[25]

25 B. Pollock, a business card and a bill head. The invoice is for 28 March 1913

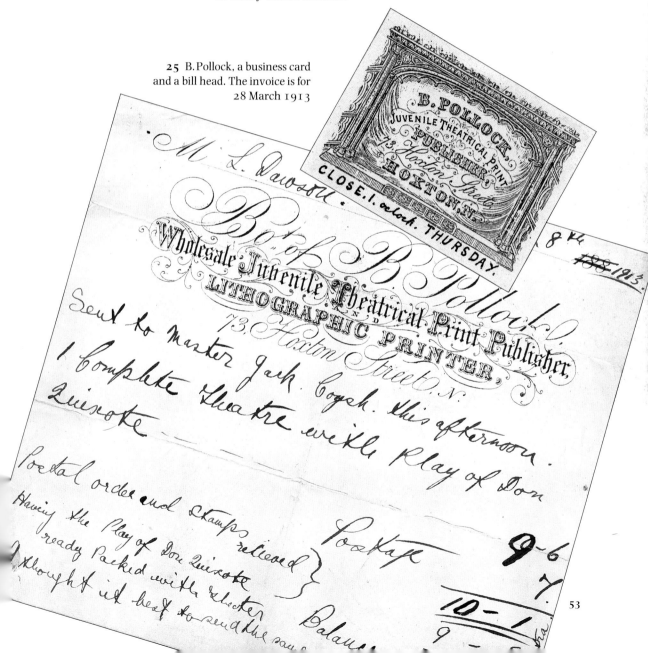

The rigours of running the shop finally proved too great and Benjamin Pollock died in August 1937 aged eighty-one. The following year Louisa put the shop up for sale, together with the 1000 or so copper plates still remaining. A letter of the same date reveals a formidable amount of stock-taking:

60 Drawings on stone for large scenes, Orchestras, Drop Scenes etc.	£30.00.0
14,533 Printed Books of Words 8/4d per 100	£60.11.1
166,460 Small plain sheets for the plays and various odd sheets 3/- per 100	£249.13.6
13,270 Single plain figures 3/– per 100	£19.17.6
6,890 Large plain scenes 6/– per 100	£20.13.6
	EXTRA £30.00.0
	£410.15.7 [26]

However, Selina and Louisa had to wait until 1944 before an advertising man called Alan Keen finally bought the entire stock for little over what the sisters had valued it at in 1938.

It was a fortunate move: no sooner had the stock been removed than a doodlebug fell nearby, all but destroying the building (Fig 26).

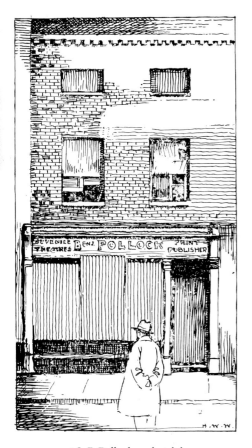

26 B. Pollock, a sketch by H. W. Whanslaw of Pollock's shop prior to its final demolition in the early 1950s. Whanslaw was a founder member of the British Model Theatre Guild

Benjamin Pollock Limited (1946-52)

Having abandoned advertising in favour of the antiquarian book trade, Alan Keen set about re-establishing Pollock's toy theatre business (Fig 27).

Keen made the acquaintance of George Speaight who, for several Christmas's before the Second World War, had performed toy theatre plays at Bumpus's, the famous Oxford Street bookshop (Fig 28).

27 Benjamin Pollock Ltd, Alan Keen the antiquarian bookseller, who bought Pollock's entire stock in 1944 and re-established the business in 1946

28 Benjamin Pollock Ltd, a toy theatre performance of *The Sleeping Beauty* by George Speaight at Bumpus's bookshop in Oxford Street, as depicted by Steven Spurrier in *The Illustrated London News*, 1935

THE DESIGNS

It was not surprising therefore that Keen should ask Speaight to join him in his venture. Between them they established Benjamin Pollock Limited in 1946 at smart premises in the Adelphi. To celebrate this event they produced a series of modernized, colour-printed theatres, including a wood and bakelite stage front with the *Adelphi* proscenium (Fig 29).

Besides selling off old stock from Hoxton, Keen and Speaight reproduced a number of plays in colour – *The Silver Palace, Aladdin, Cinderella* and *Blackbeard the Pirate* – as well as commissioning new plays. *The High Toby*, a tale of highwaymen, was written by J.B. Priestley and designed by the distinguished stage designer Doris Zinkeisen.

29 Benjamin Pollock Ltd, *The Adelphi Theatre*, 1946

To complete the miniaturization of the toy stage, working models of real theatre lights were available. A 1947 catalogue illustrated spotlights, floodlights and colour filters ranging in price from five to sixty-three shillings (Fig 30). However, Keen's over-enthusiasm was not matched by public demand and they were forced to move to smaller premises in Little Russell Street, finally closing in 1952. Nonetheless, inspite of their failure Keen and Speaight helped to rekindle public interest in the toy theatre and assistance was soon at hand.

★ ★

Pollock's Toy Museum

Whilst seeking to buy accessories for her son's theatre, a French lady working at the BBC called Marguerite Fawdry, was surprised to discover that Keen and Speaight's business no longer existed. Subsequent inquiries led her to the receivers and with the help of her father-in-law she bought, not only the required accessories, but the entire stock. With gifts and loans from friends Marguerite Fawdry established Pollock's Toy Museum at 44 Monmouth Street, with the aim of displaying not only toy theatres, but a vast range of Victorian and Edwardian toys. The popularity of this venture soon

30 Benjamin Pollock Ltd, *Model Stage Lighting Equipment*, from the front cover of a 1947 catalogue

led to a more permanent home at number 1 Scala Street, where it continues to attract tourists, journalists and enthusiasts from all over the world.

In 1980 further premises were purchased in the newly restored Covent Garden Market where stage fronts and character sheets continue to be bought and sold.

★ ★

George Conetta and Juvenile Drama in Jersey

The world of toy theatre is filled with eccentrics, none more so than
two gentlemen who, inspite of living far apart, both published
Juvenile Drama and corresponded at length on the subject. They
were George Conetta (alias George Skelt) and A. How Mathews.

Conetta was, perhaps, the more extraordinary of the two. The son
of a clergyman, he was born and christened George Wood in 1881.
At an early age he quarrelled with his father and left home to live
with an Italian family called Conetta. During the 1920s he served
in the Army and the Merchant Navy. He finally settled in Jersey
where, having married a local girl, he established a moderately
successful scrap metal business and developed a reputation for
wearing women's clothes and large straw hats. At about the same
time he renewed a childhood interest in the Juvenile Drama which
manifested itself in the redrawing and reprinting of many of the
sheets of earlier publishers. Original copies of these sheets were
borrowed from a number of sources, including the collection of
H. C. Sage, a postman from Leyton in the East End of London.[27] It is
difficult to know exactly why Conetta did this, beyond the fact that
it was an absorbing hobby.

Claiming descent from the Skelt family, Conetta published under
the pseudonym of G. Skelt. Although his sheets were copies, they
could hardly be described as forgeries, since he made no attempt to
sell them commercially and sent only a few to friends in Australia.[28]
These are now collectors items in their own right.

THE DESIGNS

One of the few surviving stage fronts by Conetta is in the author's
private collection (Fig 31). Published in 1948, the *New Stage Front*
is far larger than any extant English stage and features an odd mix
of design elements.

A year before he died Conetta wrote an article for *The Puppet
Master*, the journal of the British Puppet and Model Theatre Guild,

XI Attr Adolf Engel, Berlin,
Opera stage front. It was imported
by Gamages of Holborn and
appeared in their 1906 catalogue.
The scene is from *Little Red
Riding Hood*

XII Oehmigke and Riemschneider, proscenium for *Papiertheater* No 4866, c1840. The design shows how basic in design German sheets were at this time, with no lower section for the front of the stage and very rarely an orchestra strip

Proscenium
Neu Ruppin, bei Oehmigke & Riemschneider.

N° 1866.

most of which deals with the history of the toy theatre. However, one section at least affords us a glimpse of the attraction Conetta felt towards the subject: '. . . of course, most people will say this is all 1066 stuff . . . but the model stage is a worthwhile hobby and, if you take to it, will give you . . . hours of amusement'.[29]

31 G. Skelt (alias Conetta), *New Stage Front*, 1948

★ ★

A. How Mathews and Juvenile Drama in Acton

Conetta's correspondent in Churchfield Road, Acton was the musician and organist, A. How Mathews. Publishing between 1886 and 1906, his sheets were simply retitled copies of designs by Park, Skelt, Green and Webb.

THE DESIGNS

Mathews's largest proscenium – *Large Stage* – was an amalgam of several earlier fronts by other publishers (Pl VII). The boxes and their occupants were from Redington's *New and Improved* theatre (cf Fig 2 1), the top right box being a direct copy. The pediment was inspired of Webb's large theatre (cf Fig 1 8). For all this Mathews was a superb colourist. He had a genuine flair for mixing and applying basic powders and achieved convincing results in the traditional style (Pl VII).

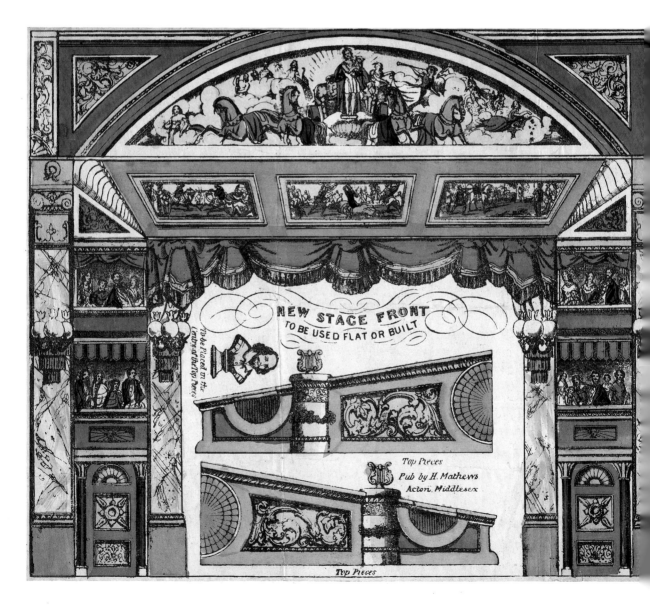

One of Mathews's most beautiful designs was the slightly smaller
New Stage Front (Fig 34). It was almost a direct copy of a twopenny
front published by W. G. Webb except that it had fewer occupants in
the boxes. The left- and right-hand panels over the arch showed
exactly the same vignette of William Tell shooting at the apple on
his son's head, although Mathews replaced George and the Dragon
on the centre panel with jousting figures. Likewise, on the pediment
Mars was removed in favour of the gentler Apollo. The orchestra –
chamber rather than full-scale pit – was cribbed from an earlier
B. Pollock design (cf Pl VI).

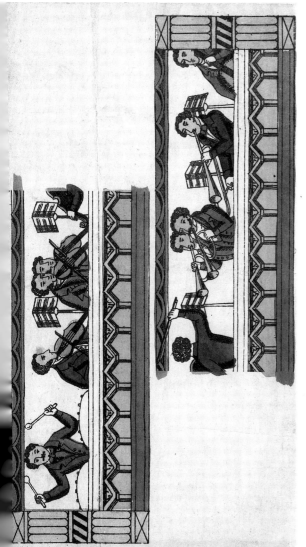

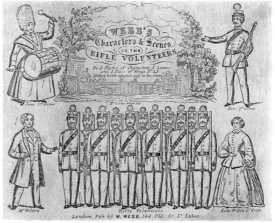

32 and **33** A. H. Mathews,
title sheets from Webb's *Rifle
Volunteers* and Mathews's *Cheer,
Boys, Cheer* respectively

34 A. H. Mathews, *New Stage
Front*, twopenny sheet form

★ ★

H.G.Clarke and the penny packet publishers in London

Conetta, Mathews, Webb and Pollock were all attempting to preserve the traditional Juvenile Drama. However, by the end of the nineteenth century this had almost completely vanished. Nevertheless, small printing firms and stationers decided there was still a market and kept the toy theatre alive by producing very cheap and poorly produced sheets. In many cases these were unsuitable for practical purposes: one sheet would contain all the necessary scenery, text and characters to be incorporated with a stage as little as a foot high. The most prolific and business-like of these cheaper publishers was in Covent Garden. In his exhortation to 'speed to Pollock's', Robert Louis Stevenson added, 'or to Clarke's of Garrick Street'.[30]

H.G.Clarke not only acted as agent for Webb and Pollock, but also produced his own stages, 'midget' plays, panoramas and 'Galanty' shows. A good idea of his stock-in-trade is provided by a scene sheet from one of his plays showing the shop in Garrick Street (Fig 35). The *Galanty Show* displayed in the front window contained the classic shadow play, *The Broken Bridge*.

THE DESIGNS

The most impressive of Clarke's theatres was the *Large Theatre Proscenium* (Fig 36). Inspite of its appearance it was not based on any specific contemporary building, although the figures at the bottom were taken from the burlesque *Bombastes Furioso*, first performed at The Haymarket Theatre in 1810. Other penny packet publishers who came and went include, Bishops of Houndsditch (c1870), S.Marks and Sons (c1880), Goode Brothers of Clerkenwell (c1890) and the publisher of the *Globe Theatre*. The latter was something of an oddity: despite the English sounding name it was printed in Germany and bore no relation to Shakespeare's theatre.

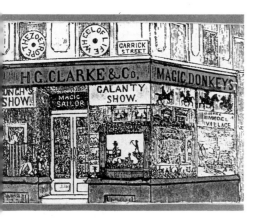

35 H.G.Clarke,
Number 2 Garrick Street, a
pantomime backcloth to one
of his 'midget' plays

36
H.G.Clarke, *Large Theatre Proscenium*,
sheet size 44 × 57cm, c1880

H.G.CLARKE & CO.   2 GARRICK STREET COVENT GARDEN

28   29   30   27   26   25   24   23   22

★ ★

Penny Packet publishers in the provinces

The toy theatre trade was mostly confined to London. However there were outposts operating in the provinces.

During the late 1880s C. Clark of 53 Temple Street, Manchester offered his Juvenile Dramas for a penny each (Fig 37). In Liverpool, James Gage, newsagent, printer and stationer, operated just around the corner from the Alexandra Theatre and the Opera House, at 10 Pembroke Place. Here he produced a few cheaply printed sheets including *The Black Pirate*, based very loosely on the story of Blackbeard.

37 C. Clark, envelope for Juvenile Drama sheets, *c*1888

38
Yates and Company, proscenium, *c*1890

Between 1880 and 1890, slightly more sophisticated Juvenile Drama sheets were produced in Nottingham by Yates and Company (owners John and Joseph Johnson) of Old Radford Works, Ilkeston Road. Many of these, including an impressive design for a proscenium (*c*1890), look as if they might have been influenced by German toy theatres (Fig 38, cf Ch 2, p 79 ff). The characters in Fig 38 are not in the traditional English style, although the orchestra is and suggests the influence of Webb. Local directories of the

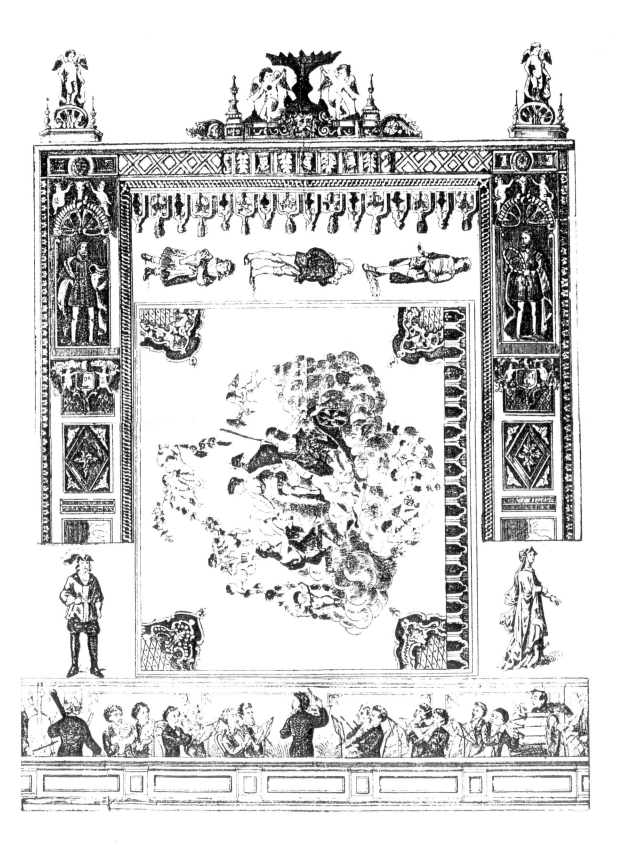

1880s list Yates and Company as lithographers, colour printers and makers of transparent plates. It may well be they only turned to the sale of toy theatre sheets after establishing links with the German trade in the early years of this century.[31]

Given away with number one

During the 1860s another facet of the Juvenile Drama began to emerge. In essence this consisted of giving away free sheets of scenes and characters as an inducement for boys to buy magazines containing adventure stories, travel tales and 'how to make your own' guides. Juvenile magazines – generally of a rather pious nature – had been published since the late eighteenth century; by the 1830s they had become very popular reading.

However, 1865 saw the arrival of a new magazine, *Black Eyed Susan*, published by the Temple Publishing Company, together with the announcement that a 'monstre [sic] sheet of scenes and characters will be presented gratis to all purchasers of No 1'. The play, a traditional one, was *The Red Rover* (Fig 39). This was probably the first offer of its kind. Unfortunately there is no evidence to show how successful it was.

39 Temple Publishing Company, *The Red Rover* title sheet, 1865

XIII Oehmigke and Riemschneider, character sheet for *Die Jungfrau von Orleans*, c1840

Die Jungfrau von Orleans.

Johanna d'Arc.   Carl VII.   Isabeau.   Philipp der Gute.   Dunois.

La Hire.   Du Chatel.   Chatillon.   Thibaut.   Talbot.

Agnes Sorel.   Johanna d'Arc.   Raimond.   Lionel.   Soldat.

No. 7051.   Neu-Ruppin, bei Oehmigke & Riemschneider.

XV Joseph Scholz, *Proscenium No 7*, c1880

XVI J.F.Schreiber, large
proscenium, showing a rare
example of an orchestra on a
continental sheet with child
players in Hanoverian costume

★ ★

Boys of England

However, the following year another boys' journal was launched which was to prove highly successful. In 1866 Charles Stevens launched *Boys of England*, a 'young gentleman's journal' dedicated to 'Sport, Travel, Fun and Instruction' which included as its first gripping story *Alone in the Pirates' Lair*, together with a sheet of figures for a toy theatre version of the tale. The intention was to gradually give away the entire story with subsequent numbers of

40 Edwin J. Brett, re-issued front page of Volume I, Number I of *Boys of England*, 1867

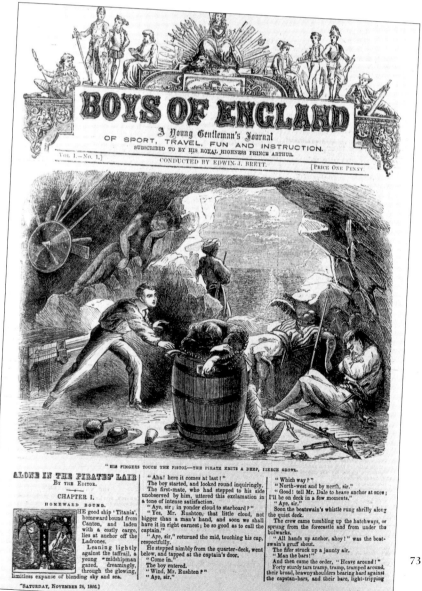

the publication. Stevens was succeeded as proprietor by Edwin J. Brett, who remained in charge for the next fourteen years. Brett, the son of an army officer, had begun his journalistic career as an illustrator and while he pursued other interests, most notably his passion for arms and armour, it is as a magazine proprietor that he is best known today.

Such was the popularity of *Boys of England*, that within a year of its inception Brett had re-issued the original front cover story (Fig 40). Other tales were dramatized and presented in a similar way as demand for the printed sheets increased. Indeed, on publication day – half-past one on a Friday – Brett's offices would become so crowded with boys clamouring for the next set of story sheets, that the police often had to be called to keep the peace.

THE DESIGNS

Brett's second play was adapted from the story of *Jack Cade or the Rebel of London*. It contained seven large scenes, eight sheets of characters, a splendid new stage front (Fig 41), an orchestra, a sheet of mechanical effects and two sheets of side wings. Jack Cade – the leader of a 1450 peasant uprising against the high taxation of Henry VI – provided readers with a suitably dashing hero.

Brett's intention was to create a complete package supplying wooden stages on which to mount his sheets and plays. In an advertisement entitled *The Stage! The Stage!* Brett announced that he had, 'great pleasure in informing . . . readers that we are now making arrangements to supply them with large stages suitable for the new play "Alone in the Pirates' Lair" also with a large front

41 Edwin J. Brett,
Boys of England stage front

42 Edwin J. Brett,
The Stage! The Stage!, advertisement
from *Boys of England*, issue 15,
4 March 1867

THE STAGE! THE STAGE!

Price 1s. 3d., or 15 stamps.

Our Theatres will be strongly constructed of wood by the largest stage manufacturer in London. Each Theatre will contain two *modern* sliding traps, place for lamp, roller for green curtain, grooves for back and side scenes, &c. Sawing and planing machines are employed to prepare the wood; but, as a short time must elapse before our immense orders are completed, our Readers will be wise if they send their orders at once to their Booksellers, as they will be supplied as each order is received.

After the completion of the Play "Alone in the Pirate's Lair," we shall issue other plays with the BOYS OF ENGLAND." The scenes, characters, &c., of these will be made the same size as those already issued ie order that they may fit the stage now in preparation.

N.B.—The usual price would be about 2s. for the Stage, but we have determined to supply our Boys with the Large Stage and Stage Front for 1s. 3d. The Lamps for each Stage, with six tin slides, can be had for four Stamps extra. Each Stage will have the title of the Boys of England printed on it, and our Readers are cautioned to purchase no Stage that does not bear the Proprietor's Signature—

Edwin J Brett

EDWIN J. BRETT'S NEW STAGE FRONT FOR THE BOYS OF ENGLAND: A YOUNG GENTLEMAN'S JOURNAL.

Fig. 4.

Fig. 3.

Figs. 2 and 3 to be joined and placed at the Top of Stage, with Fig. 4 for Centre.

Fig. 2.

designed and engraved expressly for our boys.' However, magazine publishing is a precarious business. Issue fifteen carried a similar advertisement announcing that, 'a short time must elapse before our immense orders are completed' (Fig 42). Finally, issue twenty-one of 13 April 1867 included an article on 'How to Make a Stage'. Apparently Brett's suppliers had let him down: the next best thing was to instruct boys on how to make their own. Further plays from Brett included old favourites like *The Forty Thieves, Blue Beard* and *The Miller and His Men*.

★ ★

Hogarth House and continental rivals

Rivals to Brett included the proprietor of Hogarth House. His *Tyburn Dick* was not, however, a success and he only published one play, *Turpin's Ride to York*, a popular subject from the Penny Dreadful papers (Fig 43). Similarly, Charles Fox dramatized *Sweeney Todd* for his magazine *The Boy's Standard* which, during its twenty year life, had a circulation approaching that of *Boys of England*.

43 Hogarth House, proscenium for *Turpin's Ride to York*, a story featured in the *Tyburn Dick* magazine, c1870

44 *Theatre With Footlights*, a German theatre model listed in a Gamages of Holborn catalogue, 1906

THEATRE, WITH FOOTIGHTS.
The best Miniature Toy Theatre in the market. Strongly made and fitted with properly working curtain, English pattern, footlights to burn oil, beautifully lithographed characters, mounted on cardboard and cut ready for use. These Theatres have complete set of characters, etc., as per book.

No.	2a	3a	5a	6a
	7/11	13/9	18/6	37/6

Postage 6d. under 20/- in value.

SPLENDID STAGE FRONT

Is Pre___t GRATI. with N.. 1 & 2 of

TYBURN DICK,

THE BOY KING OF THE HIGHWAYMEN.

CHARACTERS AND SCENES IN THE EXCITING PLAY OF

"TURPIN'S RIDE TO YORK"

Will be given away with Nos. 5, 7, 9, 11, 13, 15, 17, 19 and 21 of

TYBURN DICK.

All the Plates of Characters and Scenes will be beautifully Coloured
by Hand, ready for Mounting, forming the Complete Play.

PUBLISHING OFFICE

HOGARTH HOUSE, 32, BOUVERIE STREET, FLEET STREET, E.C.

During the last quarter of the nineteenth century English toy theatre suffered a severe set-back in the face of competition from very grand, ready-built theatres imported from Germany. The firm primarily responsible for this was Gamages toy shop, Holborn. Their 1906 catalogue listed a number of colour models, without actually stating their origin (Fig 44). Unlike their English counterparts, the stages were ready-made, complete with cut-out characters and prepared scenery.[32]

CHAPTER TWO

PAPIERTHEATER IN GERMANY

★ ★

Until it was destroyed during the Second World War, the original eighteenth-century model of the stage illustrated in Fig 45, was displayed in the National Museum in Nuremberg. Its rococo exterior houses an elaborate scene of a military encampment. Its backcloth, divided in the centre, was designed to open to reveal the heavens, part of which can be seen above enveloping an indistinct figure. It is particularly fitting that the original model was once housed in Nuremberg. The town has always been the centre of the German toy trade and it was here, at the beginning of the last century, that paper theatre sheets first developed out of the old, eighteenth-century peepshow dioramas. The most famous engraver of these was Martin Engelbrecht from Augsburg, near Munich. He produced religious, historical and architectural scenes, comprised of cut-out sections displayed one behind the other within a proscenium.

However, it wasn't until the early decades of the nineteenth century and the development of lithographic printing – the first serious rival to copper-plate engraving – that toy theatre publishing really took off in Germany. By the 1830s sheets of hand-coloured lithographs had found their way into the printsellers' shops. These early sheets mostly contained characters only and were probably not designed to be cut up for stage performances. These are now very rare and only a few examples survive. The Frank Bradley Collection in the Derby Museum contains only one early sheet, published by F. Nap Campe of Nuremberg, of a harbour scene.[1] Other early publishers in the Nuremberg area included Fechter of Guben and Löwensohn of Furth.

45 A model of an eighteenth-century German toy theatre

46 Map of Germany showing the principal centres of paper theatre production during the nineteenth century

Unlike England, where the toy theatre trade was based almost entirely in London, in Germany businesses sprang up in a number of different cities: Nuremberg, Berlin, Neuruppin, Mainz, Esslingen and Munich. Ironically, despite a variety of locations these publishers had a number of similar characteristics: many of them bought other firms' lithographic stones and simply printed the same designs under their own names. Most of these publishers very soon included theatre sheets on their lists.

J. C. Winckelmann (c1830)

One of the finest publishers of papiertheater (paper theatre) sheets in Germany was based in Berlin. In 1828 Johann Christian Winckelmann opened a lithographic business which soon began to supplement its picture postcards and children's books with a wide range of paper theatre sheets. Winckelmann originally came from Dusseldorf where he had served an apprenticeship with Arnz and Company. Arnz later came to Berlin and became a partner in Winckelmann's firm.

THE DESIGNS

Winckelmann's designs were not wholly original. According to Walter Röhler, Winckelmann's figure sheets bear striking similarities to engravings in an earlier book of costume, published in 1820 by Count von Bruhl, General Superintendent of Theatres in Berlin.[2] In general, however, the scenery (Pl IX) was based upon designs by Karl Schinkel and Martin Gropius, both distinguished architects employed in designing sets for the Berlin stage.

Adolf Engel and other Berlin Publishers

Berlin continued to be a centre for paper theatre publishing throughout the nineteenth century. Amongst the better known

47 Adolf Engel, Berlin,
stage front, c1880

were L. Steffan (1830), Carl Hellriegel (c1840), F. Guillaume (1840), E. Büttner (c1860) and Adolf Engel (c1880).

THE DESIGNS

Engel produced a number of elaborate stages during the 1880s, very often with statues installed in niches either side of the proscenium arch (Fig 47, cf Pl X). Similarly, pediments would contain imposing scenes from classical mythology.

That Engel exported his designs to England is shown by the model attributed to him in Pl XI which caught the eye of the buyer for Gamages toy shop in London. It too appeared in their 1906 catalogue, described simply as 'English pattern – the best Miniature Toy Theatre in the market' (cf Fig 44). Accompanying many of Engel's designs were a number of different plays, including *Snow White, Sleeping Beauty, William Tell* and *Little Red Riding Hood*. These were not original Engel publications but were in fact direct copies of plays originally produced by J. F. Schreiber (c1878) which were subsequently reprinted in English by Moritz Gottschalk of Marienberg, Saxony. Thus in *Little Red Riding Hood* the heroine of the original version set off to visit her grandmother in Rotendorf; the English version described her travelling to Edmonton (Pl XI).

★ ★

The Kühn Family and cheaper German publishers

Berlin publishers were thus producing high-quality, hand-coloured lithographs on fine paper. But just as I. K. Green and the Skelt family popularized the toy theatre in England by reducing the quality of their prints, so too did a number of firms operating in the German town of Neuruppin. One such publisher, spanning many years, was Gustav Kühn.

Having taken over from his father in 1815, Gustav introduced the firm to the then new process of lithographic printing. Within a few years he was printing well over a 1000 different sheets on cheap paper. Kühn also had an eye for sources of cheap labour; much of

48 Gustav Kühn, Neuruppin, *Neue Theater Decoration No 8709*, hand-coloured proscenium, *c*1835

the hand colouring was done by prison and workhouse inmates. The sheets covered a wide range of subjects – scenes from the Battle of Waterloo, hunting scenes, the Burning of Moscow, cut-out models, religious scenes and table games. Amongst these were about 140 designs for theatre proscenia, characters and sets (Fig 48). It is generally accepted that Gustav Kühn pirated his designs, particularly from Winckelmann. Being exceptionally well drawn and coloured Winckelmann's sheets were not cheap and it was Kühn's aim to bring them into the reach of a wider, less affluent, section of society.

Oehmigke and Riemschneider

The lithographic printing press of Oehmigke and Riemschneider was established in Neuruppin in 1835. Having been a bookseller in Berlin since 1807, Philip Johann Oehmigke set up another shop in Neuruppin in 1828 where he was joined by Arnold Hermann Riemschneider, who later became his partner. They published sheets similar to those of Kühn and soon outstripped the latter in terms of production. After the death of both partners the firm continued to thrive until 1920, the most recent known date for printed sheets.

49 Oehmigke and Riemschneider, proscenium for *Papiertheater No 779, c 1840*

THE DESIGNS

The Museum of Deutsches Volkskunde in Berlin has a substantial number of Oehmigke and Riemschneider sheets in its collection, including one of the earliest proscenia to be published by this firm, dating from the 1840s (Fig 49). This proscenium was followed soon afterwards by a sheet of characters for *The Merchant of Venice* (No 872).

During the 1970s the Deutsches Volkskunde reprinted an original Oehmigke and Riemschneider stage front (Fig 50), together with character sheets for the play *Hansel and Gretel*, from figure sheet Number 9769, originally published at the end of the nineteenth century.

50 Oehmigke and Riemschneider, proscenium for *Papiertheater No 4890, c 1840*. The scene is from *Faust*

51 Joseph Scholz, backdrop of cemetry, *Hamlet*, *No 201* (old series), approx 30 × 40cm, *c*1835

★ ★

Joseph Scholz of Mainz

An important centre for the production of paper theatre sheets was established in the town of Mainz. Three publishers operated here during the nineteenth century: Aleiter and Zeitinger, E. Linn and Company and, by far the most prolific, Joseph Scholz.

THE DESIGNS

During its life of nearly 130 years Scholz produced 300 different designs and a variety of stage fronts.

The company was founded in 1793 by Joseph Scholz and produced its first theatrical prints in the 1830s. These were usually character

52 Joseph Scholz,
Urania proscenium, No 8,
*c*1880

53 Joseph Scholz,
proscenium with putti and medallions
of Schiller and Goethe at either side
of the stage, *c*1880. The scene is
from *Faust*

54 Joseph Scholz,
backdrop with avenue of sphinxes,
The Magic Flute

sheets, the size of each figure varying from sheet to sheet. A typical example of Scholz's work is the character sheet for *Figaro's Hochzeit* ('Marriage of Figaro') (Pl XIV).

It was not long, however, before scenes (backdrops and wings) were issued. Some were specifically drawn for Scholz, but most were based on highly atmospheric contemporary stage designs by Karl Schinkel (Fig 51).

However, by the 1880s Scholz was no longer satisfied with reprinting extant sheets with single backcloths and flat, narrow wings. In the face of mounting competition from J.F. Schreiber of Esslingen who was printing much larger and grander scenes, Scholz commissioned Carl Beyer, the scenic artist at the Court Theatre at Darmstadt, to design a range of more complicated scenes incorporating variously shaped cut-out wings and set pieces, creating more elaborate effects (Fig 54). These fascinating scenes, or *Satz-Dekoration*, were sold as complete sets in both large and small format.

Scholz's catalogue also provided a wide choice of stage fronts all with varying sizes of proscenium (Figs 52 and 53). Many of these were extremely elegant often incorporating statuesque figures and symbolic theatrical masks in low relief, as well as suitably worried looking prompters inside shell-shaped boxes (Pl XV). New scene sheets were still being published after 1900, some designed by a Berlin scenic artist by the name of Müller. However, the First World War brought production to a halt. During the 1920s the expense of printing and hand colouring, coupled with the most appalling inflation and general lack of interest, forced the firm to pulp its remaining stock, thereby ensuring the rarity of Scholz sheets today.

★ ★

J.F. Schreiber of Esslingen

That the same fate did not befall the thousands of remaindered sheets belonging to the firm of J.F. Schreiber of Esslingen, is due largely to the forethought and quick-wittedness of Marguerite

55 J.F.Schreiber, *Rococo Proscenium*
No 400 a & b, c1894

Fawdry of Pollock's Toy Museum in London. In the late 1960s word spread that Schreiber's had ceased their toy theatre operation and that they intended to pulp a large stock of sheets dating back to the beginning of the century. Fortunately Pollock's moved in and, for an undisclosed sum, bought the lot. Upon arrival in England they were sorted out and put up for sale, initially at three pounds per 100 sheets. It was a mixed collection: there were no complete plays, but there was wide range of colour-printed character sheets, scenes and sets in two sizes (small format, 36 × 43cm and large format, 43 × 54cm). The real joy was finding a proscenium amongst the pile, still intact and with fabulous colouring (Fig 55).

Entering the toy theatre business at a rather late stage, Ferdinand Schreiber (Fig 56) had the advantage of being able to examine which areas of the market had not yet been exploited. He was thus able to improve the general presentation of the sheets and plays. These were accepted as being far superior to those of other publishers. Ferdinand Schreiber further improved the position of the firm by publishing two instruction books on how to construct all the necessary technical equipment to go with the plays. The first, *Das Kindertheater* by Hugo Elm, was published in 1886, to be followed by another in 1900 by Max Eickemeyer (Fig 57).

From the beginning Schreiber's output was extensive and highly competitive. He produced two sizes of sheets, the result of acquiring the lithographic stones of two separate companies in nearby Stuttgart. The first, Halder and Cronberger – acquired in 1850 – had produced scenery in the smaller format; the second, E. Roth – bought in 1870 – had published large format scenery. Having obtained the stones Schreiber merely applied his own imprint.

THE DESIGNS AND THE WORK OF THEODOR GUGGENBERGER

Schreiber aimed at a young market; the character sheets – of which there were about eighty – show a preference to children's stories. Usually there was only one character sheet to a play; *Aschenbrödel* ('Cinderella'), *Round the World in Eighty Days* and *The Fairy Doll* were the notable exceptions. Moreover, there was generally only one design per character, so the leading performers would have to go the entire length of a play standing rigidly in one position.

56 Ferdinand Schreiber (1835-1914), son of Johann Ferdinand Schreiber, the original founder of the firm

57 Max Eickemeyer, *Das Kindertheater*, published by J. F. Schreiber, 1900

XVII J.F. Schreiber, *Temple of Isis* scene sheet for *The Magic Flute*, *c*1890. This scene sheet is notable for the enormous attention paid to detail, especially the accurate hieroglyphics on the walls and columns

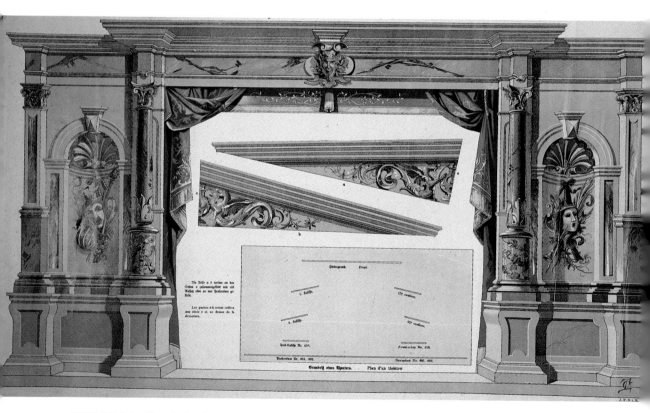

XVIII J.F. Schreiber, design by
Guggenberger for a proscenium
(*No 401/402*)

XIX J.F. Schreiber, proscenium design (*Noa & b*) by Guggenberger, *c*1890. The two equestrian figures are based on two similar ones adorning the Vienna State Opera

XX Diorama of the Tivoli Gardens, showing
the famous Pantomime Theatre

XXI J.F.Schreiber, *Large Theatre*
No 301. The scene is *A Japanese
Garden* from Sievert's *Der Mikado*

93

ALADDIN.

Alfred Jacobsens Danske Teaterdekorationer Nr. 175.
Carl Larsen.
Köbmagergade 40. Köbenhavn K.

Ringens Aand.

Morgiane.

Aladdin.

Soliman.

Abdul.

Gulnare.

Aladdin som Prins

Lampens Aand.

Noureddin.

Slavinde.

XXII A. Jacobsen, character sheet
for *Aladdin* from series 'F',
71 × 55 cm, 1912

XXIII A. Jacobsen, moorish-style proscenium from
series 'F', 71 × 55 cm, 1912

Plate 14.

Vienna: M. Trentsensky
Theat. Cost. 188.

COSTUMES IN SHAKSPEARE'S HISTORICAL PLAY OF

KING HENRY THE EIGHTH

Published by the kind permission of Charles Kean, Esq.
London: A. & S. Joseph, Myers & Cº

Plate 15

Vienna: M. Trentsensky
Theat. Cost. 189

COSTUMES IN SHAKSPEARE'S HISTORICAL PLAY OF

KING HENRY THE EIGHTH

Published by the kind permission of Charles Kean, Esq.
London: A. & S. Joseph, Myers & Cº

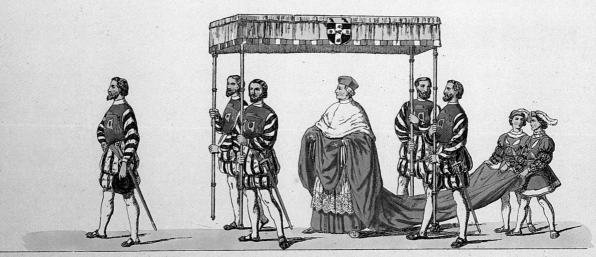

Plate 3

Vienna: M. Trentsensky
Theat. Cost. 177

COSTUMES IN SHAKSPEARE'S HISTORICAL PLAY OF

KING HENRY THE EIGHTH

Published by the kind permission of Charles Kean, Esq.
London: A. & S. Joseph, Myers & Cº

The early sheets were all hand-coloured and the scenes were purely generic: *Wood, Garden, Town, Room, Village* etc. The playbooks would list which scenes were to be used from this stock to match particular plays, usually giving the numbers of the large and small format sheets. Later, however, specific scenes were published such as *Oriental Garden* and *Temple of Isis* for *The Magic Flute* (Pl XVII).

By the end of the 1880s Ferdinand Schreiber had acquired the services of the noted Munich stage designer, Theodor Guggenberger (Fig 58).

Guggenberger gradually replaced the old series of sheets with new and more elaborate ones. His first design for Schreiber was an elegant proscenium published in 1888, when he was just twenty-two (Pl XVIII). The design shows immense care and attention to detail, and in many ways strongly reflects the court theatres and castle decoration of Ludwig II. This is not altogether surprising, as Guggenberger studied under Angelo Quaglio, junior court painter to Ludwig.

Guggenberger's work for Schreiber was prolific. The archives at the Schreiber factory in Esslingen contain nearly fifty of his original designs in water-colour and tempera, together with information on the fees he was paid for each design:

The Warrior's Tent (No 673) 80 Marks

Lichenstein Backdrop (No 135) 40 Marks

Thorn Hedge (No 664/5) 35 Marks

Charcoal Burner's hut, section of set pieces 6 Marks

Barrel 2.50 Marks

This was at a time when a postman's average monthly wage was just 100 Marks. [3]

THE TEXTS

One of the earliest text writers for Schreiber's plays was Ernst Sievert. In 1880 he published a book, *Theater in der Kinderstube*, which contained the first nine plays in Schreiber's repertoire. In his

58 Theodor Guggenberger (1866-1929), stage designer to the Munich Theatre, who designed and redesigned scene sheets for J.F.Schreiber

XXIV M.Trentsensky, character sheet for *Henry VIII*

introduction he wrote that the plays were originally intended for use by his children and their friends on his own theatre. However, the texts did not always reflect the limitations of cardboard characters. In *Der Mikado* (a play by Sievert only loosely connected with the Gilbert and Sullivan operetta), certain passages requiring the hero to pursue the villain 'with poisoned glances', or 'to clasp his father's breast', would have defeated even the most resourceful toy theatre player (Pl XXI).

The Austrian writer, Innocens Tallavania (1868-1934) did, however, have experience of performance on a small stage having written and adapted classical plays and opera for his own toy theatre at his house in Linz's Walterstrasse.[4] Consequently his texts were more practical and were published by Schreiber. Between 1897 and 1914, Tallavania appears to have been commissioned by Schreiber to write texts for at least eighteen of the later plays: Numbers 40-53, 56-58, 60 and 63.

★ ★

Schmidt and Romer of Leipzig

Several years later, a firm in Leipzig began producing work similar to Schreiber's, though not on such a large scale. One of their most successful designs – more in the style of Joseph Scholz than Schreiber – was an elaborate proscenium called the *Thalia*, after the Muse of Comedy (Fig 59).

The output of toy theatres throughout Germany during the nineteenth century was considerable and several publishers made serious efforts to export their designs to other countries where the toy theatre was known to be popular. G. Kühn and Oehmigke and Riemschneider in particular managed to tap the Danish market, until native Danish publications superseded them in the late 1860s.

59 Schmidt and Romer, *Thalia* proscenium, *c*1890. The monstrous shell-like prompter's box is an unusual element and must have concealed much of the action on the stage

CHAPTER THREE

DUKKETEATER IN DENMARK

The history of the toy theatre (Dukketeater) in Denmark falls into four main periods: pre-Jacobsen (*c*1830-80); Alfred Jacobsen (1880-1924); the theatres of the *Illustrated Family Journal* (1914-31) and the *Pegasus Theatre* of Carl Allers (1941-49).

Thereafter, scene and character sheets, mostly from the Jacobsen and Allers periods, were reprinted and successfully sold by Vilhelm Prior's old bookshop in Copenhagen's Købmagergade. Prior's son, Aage, kept the business going until his death in 1936, when his sisters, Anne and Estrid, took over. Although the bookshop was forced to close down in 1964, Estrid Prior continued to publish and sell toy theatre sheets under the new name of *Prior's Dukketeater*. In 1976 she handed the shop over to Egon Petersen, who transformed it into a thriving business (Fig 60). Unfortunately he died in 1985, leaving his wife, Hanne, and daughter, Helle, to keep the shop going in the shadow of Copenhagen's famous Round Tower.

60 Egon Petersen and Hanne Nelander in Prior's bookshop in Copenhagen, 1984

61 Denmark, toy theatre of wood and glass, 28 × 40 cm, *c*1840

Pre-Jacobsen (*c*1830-80)

Toy theatres were not unknown in Denmark before 1830. Hans Christian Anderson (b 1805) spent much of his childhood playing with them. An awkward and unhappy youth, Anderson occupied long hours recreating his favourite stories on the stage of his miniature theatre, frequently performing them to local children.

Having failed both to become an actor and a playwright in Copenhagen, Anderson returned to the fairy tales of his youth through which he would eventually become internationally famous. In one of these, *The Money Box*, Anderson featured his toy theatre in an episode where the grand Piggy Bank Pig sits high upon a cupboard, while the rest of the playthings sit below watching a comedy on a small stage:

The play was worthless, but well acted. All the actors turned their painted side to the audience, for they were never meant to be seen from the wrong side. They acted splendidly, right out in front of the floodlights, for their wires were a little too long, but then they could be seen all the better for that.

Unfortunately, in all the excitement, the grand Piggy fell and was smashed to pieces.

Anderson's theatre and plays were probably made especially for him. However, by 1830, C. Steen of Copenhagen was producing character sheets on a commercial basis. Like Germany, many of these early sheets were possibly only intended as costume plates, or portraits of well-known actors and actresses on the Copenhagen stage. George Garde illustrates several examples of early sheets showing portraits taken from C. Bruun and characters from Holberg's comedies.[1]

THE DESIGNS

One of the earliest surviving Danish toy theatres is held by the National Museum in Copenhagen (Fig 61). Dating from about 1840, it is a home-made model of wood and glass with ornate inlaid decoration and contains three backcloth sheets, three wing-pieces and a narrow backdrop and front cloth. All of these are colour-printed and were probably imported from Germany by Blankensteiners bookshop in Copenhagen.[2]

The National Museum also holds a more elaborate Danish toy theatre, again dating from the first half of the nineteenth century (Fig 62) and much more in the traditional style than Fig 61. One of its most notable features is the complicated structure behind the proscenium, which allowed for flying scenery, a trapdoor in the

62 Denmark, toy theatre, wood, *c*1840

stage and the fixing of candle lights in such a way that they could be simultaneously rotated by pulling on a string. Above the arch there is a motto which reads, 'For the Encouragement to Unceasing Industry'. The theatre was commissioned by Pastor Johann Frederick Tøpsoe, from Master Painter Jorgensen, for his nine-year-old son, who later became a priest himself. Interestingly, the theatre also incorporates a German drop-curtain, by Winckelmann of Berlin. Until the Prusso-Danish War of 1864, it was quite normal to find Danish bookshops importing German sheets, especially those of Kühn and Oehmigke and Riemschneider of Neuruppin. However, after the war public attitudes changed, and anything of German origin, including toy theatre sheets, was widely boycotted.

By the 1870s, Danish firms such as E. O. Jordan of Copenhagen were publishing characters, scenes and text for popular plays like *Round the World in Eighty Days*, which was currently enjoying great success at the city's Casino Theatre. Other publishing houses to include toy theatre sheets among their products were August I. Wolff, Theodor Mathiesen and Michaelsen and Tilge, who published a stage front based upon Copenhagen's Royal Theatre bearing the motto *Ei Blot Til Lyst* ('Not only for Pleasure'). This was to become the trade mark of the theatres of Alfred Jacobsen.

★ ★

Alfred Jacobsen (1880-1924)

In 1873 Alfred Jacobsen opened a lithographic printers, so beginning the second, great period of Danish toy theatre history. Jacobsen, a particularly virulent xenophobe and anti-German, embarked upon a crusade to ensure that Danish children had Danish pictures. On the 7 February 1880, from his flat in Copenhagen's Lovstraede, he published the first issue of a magazine called *Soufløren* ('The Prompter') which aimed to introduce children to the pleasures of the toy theatre, using a heavy mixture of indoctrination and anti-German imagery. Jacobsen began by telling the story of a group of children whose initial attempts at producing a play on a German toy theatre end in disaster. The kindly 'Prompter' comes to their rescue and tells them how to build their own, far superior, theatre. Included in the first issue was a proscenium sheet to be placed in front of the stage.

THE DESIGNS

Jacobsen's first theatre was an extremely complicated structure and would have probably defeated even the most intelligent of Danish children (Figs 63 and 64). It incorporated an intricate system of wires for changing the wings and altering the gelatines in front of the candles (Fig 64), as well as having a roller curtain and stage trapdoor.

While Jacobsen designed many of the proscenia and curtains for the plays himself, he also commissioned artists such as J. C. Deickmann and Peter Klaestrup to do the characters and scenery. *The Prompter* continued for twenty-four editions, each containing sheets of scenes and characters together with proscenia of various sizes. Jacobsen was an adept businessman and advertised his magazine extensively on posters around Copenhagen. These were usually next to advertisements for stage plays, as well as on the boards of the Tivoli Gardens, a popular summer pleasure-ground (Pl XX).

By the end of 1881 the first edition of twelve issues was complete. It sold for fifty øre (about three and a half pence). Worried that the price might be too expensive for children, Jacobsen instituted an instalment system; later he provided twenty-five øre saving stamps to be stuck into books which, when filled, would pay for a theatre. Growing success enabled Jacobsen to move to grander premises on the corner of Købmagergade, where he built a case to display his stage, character and scene sheets. He also commissioned the well-known illustrator and costume designer, Carsten Ravn to design the figures for *Kejserens Kurer* ('Michael Strogoff') and many other productions over the following thirty-two years until Ravn's death in 1914.

During the first four years of what became known as the 'old' series, some eighteen plays were published on seventy sheets of figures, backdrops, wings and sets. Titles included adaptations of popular Parisian shows such as *Orpheus and the Underworld* and

63 A. Jacobsen, toy theatre built in accordance with the instructions in the first issue of *Soufløren*, 1880. The proscenium, together with the motto on the pediment, was based upon Copenhagen's Royal Theatre

64 Detail of Fig 63

XXV M. Trentsensky, backcloth,
moonlit scene

THÉÂTRE FRANÇAIS

COMÉDIE

DRAME

PELLERIN & Cⁱᵉ IMP.-ÉDIT.

IMAGERIE D'ÉPINAL FONDÉE EN 1796

65 A. Jacobsen, proscenium from the new 'C' series, 90 × 65 cm, 1884. The loggia design was taken almost entirely from the Royal Theatre

XXVI Imagerie Pellerin, *Devanture* No 1541, *Théâtre Français*, This well-known design incorporated boxes, an orchestra and detailed instructions on how to construct the stage (cf Fig 78). The *Commedia dell'Arte* figures are of moulded tin, based on designs by Maurice Sand and made in Nurnberg, Germany

Prins Pipi og Frøken Titi, currently enjoying a renaissance at the Casino Theatre. There were also patriotic plays taken from the Casino's adaptations of popular novels, including *Tordenskjold* (a naval hero from the Swedish Wars) and *Valdemar Sejr* ('King Valdemar').

In 1884 a larger series of proscenia was launched, inaugurated by the publication of a more elaborate proscenium, still based on the Royal Theatre, but containing a more formal design on the base (Fig 65).

Other stage sizes quickly followed: series 'D' (just 35×39 cm) in 1892 and series 'A', the largest (106×80 cm), in 1906 (Fig 66). 1912 saw the launch of a new, smaller stage size (the 'F' series) heralded by the publication of an elegant moorish proscenium and character sheet for an adaptation of *Aladdin* (Pls XXII and XXIII).

Whereas the characters of Jacobsen's plays were often recognizable as real-life actors on the Copenhagen stage (the designer would often work from a photograph), the scenery tended to be taken from a permanent stock of woods, gardens, towns etc. Occasionally special sets were drawn, most notably those for Jacobsen's adaptation of the Casino's production of *Michael Strogoff*, one of which was an interior view of the Paris Opera (Fig 67). Most of Jacobsen's plays were light-weight fairy stories, adaptations of Casino plays and patriotic pieces; he published very little serious drama and only six of his plays are known to be from the lists of the Royal Theatre. Inspite of this, however, by the time he died in 1924 Jacobsen had created a magical toy theatre world, uniquely Danish in design and spirit and far removed from either the German Papiertheater, or the English Juvenile Drama.

66 A. Jacobsen, proscenium from the largest 'A' series, 106×80 cm, 1906

67 A. Jacobsen, Paris Opera backdrop from *Michael Strogoff*, c 1886

★ ★

Theatres of the *Illustrated Family Journal* (1914-31)

For a number of years prior to Jacobsen's death the Copenhagen publisher Carl Allers had been producing a very popular magazine, the *Illustrated Family Journal* (Fig 68), which contained pages of models for children to cut out and make. In 1914, as a result of the success of Jacobsen's venture, Allers decided to incorporate a toy theatre with each issue of his magazine.

THE DESIGNS

The first theatre was a modest affair (Fig 69). The design did, however, extend the proscenium forward so that part of the audience and orchestra could be seen and the boxes were suitably crowded for the opening production of *Den Fortryllede Princesse* ('The Bewitched Princess'). This idea was so successful that Allers not only published a new theatre design, but also brought out a Swedish and Norwegian edition in the space of a year. A total of six different plays were published in successive weekly editions, necessitating the purchase of a complete volume in order to obtain a full play with stage front.

For seventeen years the magazine flourished. There was a new theatre design almost every year (Figs 70 and 71), ranging in size

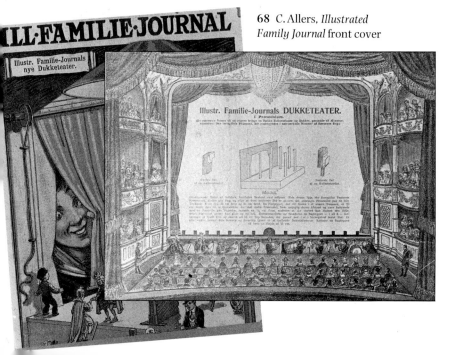

68 C. Allers, *Illustrated Family Journal* front cover

69 C. Allers, *Illustrated Family Journal*, the first toy theatre, 27 × 38 cm, 1914

ANNO MCMXVIII

70 C. Allers,
Illustrated Family Journal,
large theatre, 1918

from the small *Lilleput* (8 × 14 cm) in 1916, to an amazingly large
Sammenklappelig theatre, with scenery measuring 64 × 45 cm,
in 1927. This required several pages of magazine to make up the
stage front.

★ ★

Carl Allers and the *Pegasus Theatre*

By 1930, however, times were changing and public interest in cut-
out models was on the wane. In 1931 the *Illustrated Family Journal*
discontinued publication of theatres and plays.

71 C. Allers,
Illustrated Family Journal, theatre,
1925

72 C. Allers, *Pegasus Theatre*,
1941

Not that the Allers establishment completely forgot the success toy
theatre had once enjoyed. In 1941 it brought out a new, quite
separate, theatre called the *Pegasus*, incorporating a yellow pegasus
emblazoned on a vivid blue proscenium (Fig 72). Several handbooks
were also published to help aspiring performers make the most of
the theatre including *The Model Theatre Handbook, Building
instructions for the Pegasus Theatre, The Model Theatre Painter* and
New Modern Proscenia. The last play in the *Pegasus* series, *Ringen*,
was published in 1951.

★ ★

CHAPTER FOUR

THE KINDERTHEATER
IN AUSTRIA

★ ★

Matthias Trentsensky

Matthias Trentsensky was born in Vienna in 1790. The following
year witnessed the first performance of Mozart's *The Magic Flute* at
the city's Theater auf der Wieden. Some thirty years later
Trentsensky published his character and scene sheets for the toy
theatre version of this opera. They gave an accurate picture of the
style of theatre decor at that time and were probably designed by
Theodor Jachimovitz, stage designer at the Josefstadt Theatre (later
at the State Opera), who drew most of Trentsenky's scene sheets.
Trentsenky's long association with the toy theatre began in 1819,
when he established a lithographic printing business in his native
Vienna. As a former army officer with a pension, Trentsensky was
unable to use his own name in business, so many of the early
sheets bear the name of his brother, Joseph (Fig 73).

THE DESIGNS

Apart from the usual images of soldiers, religious subjects, costume
plates and children's games, Trentsensky published two basic stage
designs: the large (*Grosses*) theatre, requiring 40 × 50 cm sheets

73 Joseph Trentsensky,
Matthias's brother

74 M. Trentsenksy,
Das Grosses Theater, c1840.
The drop-curtain showing Apollo
in a classical landscape, was
a copy of the curtain at the
Old Burg Theatre in Vienna

(Fig 74) and the little (*Mignon*) theatre designed for 20 × 30 cm sheets (Fig 75). With these stages came a wide range of elegantly designed drop-curtains and scenery. Trick scenes, in which castles turned into cottages and trees divided to reveal heavenly scenes, were a speciality.

Altogether, forty-one plays were published for the large theatre and sixteen for the little. They were based on operas, Austrian tales and Shakespeare plays. The latter were exported to England through a London agent, Myers and Company. A particularly good example, shows costume details from an 1855 production of *Henry VIII* by Charles Kean at the Princesses Theatre in Oxford Street (Pl XXIV). While many of Trentsenksy's character sheets were undoubtedly for performing purposes, a significant number were designed simply as costume plates. The layout of these was in a form peculiar to Trentsensky: just one line of figures on a 36 × 19.5 cm sheet.

Later Trentsensky designs included an elaborate stage front, still incorporating the familiar trefoil proscenium, originally with an elegant pediment adorned with swan motifs (Fig 76).

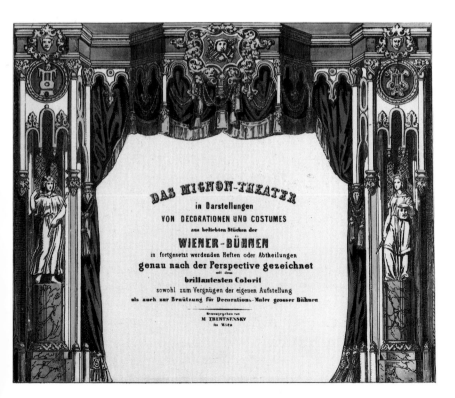

75 M. Trentsensky, *Das Mignon Theater*, c1840

76 M. Trentsensky, large stage front, c1860.

Although there were other publishers operating in Austria during the nineteenth century (Barth, Freytag and Berndt, Levy and Mossbeck for example), in terms of quality of output, none ever came close to matching Trentsensky.

PLANCHER

Il faut coller la base de la façade du théâtre contre cette partie.

THÉÂTRE FRANÇAIS

EXPLICATION

Toutes les lignes ponctuées ou se trouve le signe x sont à entailler
au dos. Tous les N° correspondants doivent être collés ensemble. Il
faut faire des incisions aux places marquees d'un trait noir ▬▬▬

CHAPTER FIVE

IMAGERIE FRANÇAIS

Imagerie Pellerin of Epinal

On the banks of the Moselle in the small town of Epinal in north-eastern France, stands the workshop of Pellerin, an old printing company founded by Jean-Charles Pellerin in 1796.

Pellerin initially began by producing cheap, hand-coloured wood-block prints of fairy tales, broadside ballads and religious subjects. During the Napoleonic era the firm established a reputation for producing numerous prints of the Emperor and his exploits. However, it was not until the middle of the nineteenth century, and the arrival of a lithographic printer from Weissembourg called M. Grivel, that Pellerin developed the concept of designing and printing toy theatres. Grivel introduced, not only the new lithographic printing process, but also cut-out card models and construction sheets.

Ironically, in France the toy theatre developed in a vacuum and, unlike the English, German and Danish toy theatre, it established no distinct tradition of drawing upon contemporary stage drama. Epinal was not a theatrical centre; it was also a long way from Paris. The children of the Vosges region knew little about the capital, let alone its glittering theatrical life. Their experience of the stage probably extended no further than the crude puppetry of the *Guignol* performers who roamed the French countryside. All the more extraordinary, therefore, that the Pellerin family produced such a wide range of stage fronts and scenes. Even so, those that were printed generally bore no relation to specific plays. Walter Röhler, the German collector, believed that the practice was instead to imitate the spirit of the *Commedia dell'Arte*.[1] Even René Perrout's

77 Imagerie Pellerin, *Petit Théâtre Lyrique*, No 1515, 12.5 × 11.5 cm. One of the designs in the *Petits Théâtres* series

78 Imagerie Pellerin, *Petit Théâtre Français*, No 98

history of *Les Images d'Epinal*, published in 1912, only mentioned Pellerin's theatre output in passing and included no illustrations.

THE DESIGNS

By the 1930s the Pellerin catalogue listed five different stage designs together with a series of character sheets:

1   *Petits Théâtres.* This was the smallest size of theatre produced by Pellerin. Four different proscenia were printed on one sheet measuring 39 × 49 cm, each with an accompanying scene: *Théâtre Guignol, Théâtre Français, Opéra* and *Théâtre Lyrique* (Fig 77). A slightly larger sheet contained all the parts needed to make up another theatre in this series (Fig 78): stage front (19 × 23 cm), stage floor (12.5 cm deep), one backcloth, two pairs of wings and twelve figures (approx 5 cm high), including dancers, musicians and various spectators.

2   *Théâtre.* The second section of the Pellerin catalogue listed fourteen different backcloths (*fonds*) with corresponding wings (*coulisses*) for the larger *Théâtre*. Stage fronts (*devantures*) included the popular *Opéra Comique* (Fig 79)

3   *Théâtre: système à rainures.* This section contained no less than ten different sets (backcloths and wings) for use with an elaborate stage front incorporating allegories of comedy and drama above the proscenium arch, based on the popular *Théâtre Français* (Pl XXVI). The stage was advertised as being available hand-coloured or, for twice the price (one franc), gilded. The sets were made up of stock scenes such as *Palais, Campagne, Palais de Luxembourg, Prison, Forêt, Salon* etc., together with generalized figures for *Comédie* and *Personnages des rues de Paris.*

4   *Théâtre doré ou non doré.* Seven sets were provided for use with this large, 45 × 61 cm stage front (Pl XXVII), available with or without gilding (*doré ou non doré*). Backcloths and wings were again taken from a permanent stock of *Forêt, Campagne, Port de Mer* etc.

79 Imagerie Pellerin,
Devanture et fond Place Publique,
Opéra Comique, No 1540

80 Imagerie Pellerin, *Grand Théâtre Nouveau, Opéra* stage front, *c*1889

5 *Grand Théâtre Nouveau*. The largest size of theatre produced by Pellerin was the *Grand Théâtre Nouveau*, which featured a number of stage fronts, including an extremely impressive *Opéra* proscenium, published in 1889 for the Paris World Exhibition (Fig 80). The large scale of the front was underlined by its classical architecture and statues of Corneille and Molière either side of the stage. In spite of the *Opéra* title, no provision was made for an orchestra in the building instructions printed on the sheet. Some twenty-seven sets were listed for use with the *Grand Théâtre Nouveau*, including the exotic *Pyramides d'Egypte* and *Gare de Chemin de fer* (Railway station).

6 *Character Sheets*. Section six of the Pellerin catalogue included a list of character sheets (*Costumes de Théâtre*) containing both general musicians, dancers, beggars etc., under *Personnages et costumes variés* (General characters and costumes), as well as specific figures like Don Quixote and Sancho Panza. Other characters included those from *Faust, La Tour de Nesle* (a melodrama by Dumas) and *La Muette de Portici*. Another allied section – *Costumes Divers* – contained sheets with generic titles such as *Espagnols* (Spanish), *Turcs et Orienteaux* (Turks and Oreintals) and *Français du temps de Charles VII* (French in the age of Charles VII). Being small and difficult to cut up, it would seem that these figures were not intended for performances.

The last two sections of the Pellerin catalogue – *Ombres Chinoises* and *Le Séraphin des Enfants* – dealt with the shadow theatre, an extremely popular form of miniature theatre in France.

★ ★

Albert Mericand and other French publishers

During the nineteenth century a number of rivals competed with Pellerin. In the 1860s Oliver Pinot started producing sheets similar to those of Pellerin. Pinot was an employee of Pellerin's workshop who set up his own business only to be bought out by his former employer in 1888. Other French publishers included F.C. Wentzel of Weissembourg, Lorraine. He specialized in producing character

XXVII Imagerie Pellerin, large stage front, *Avant Scène*, No 1579, 45 × 61 cm. The backcloth is of the *Magasin des Étoffes* from the largest, *Grand Théâtre Nouveau*, format

XXVIII Albert Mericand,
Mon Théâtre, 1904-05. The scene
is from *Le Château Magique*

and scene sheets until he was taken over by C. Burkardt in the 1860s, who later passed the business on to R. Ackermann in 1918. Their work was in the same genre as Pellerin's; the choice of subject and style of drawing was very similar. Dehalt of Nancy was another publisher who produced some exceptionally large scenes and stage fronts during the 1890s, an example of which is in the *Musée des Arts et Traditions Populaires* in Paris.

One of the few signs of toy theatre activity in Paris appeared between 1904 and 1905 in the form of a short-lived but prolific magazine called *Mon Théâtre*. Published by Albert Mericand at 1 rue du Pont de Lodi, *Mon Théâtre: Les Jouets Illustres* was, by its own admission, 'Amusant, Instructif, Artistique'. At fifty centimes it was 'un Jouet en même temps qu'un Journal'. First and foremost, however, it was a means of providing material for the toy theatre and the first issue included a grand proscenium together with a well-designed stage structure incorporating a series of upright supports to hold wing-pieces (Pl XXVIII).

The magazine was published fortnightly. Each issue contained double-sided characters and sections of scenery for an extensive list of plays. In addition to the usual backcloth and wings, the scenery also included more substantial pieces such as stairways and balconies creating a most attractive effect.

The only other evidence for toy theatre publishing in Paris is provided by an extremely rare stage front entitled *Théâtre De La Poupée Modèle* (Doll's Theatre) (Pl XXIX). This was produced thirty years before Mericand brought out his *Mon Théâtre*, by the short-lived *Journal Des Petites Filles*.

GILDING

One of the finer aspects of the French toy theatre production is to be seen in the gilding of stage fronts, scene and character sheets. Using better-quality paper, scenes and figures received the usual hand colouring, before having gilt applied to details such as buttons, swords and other weapons, brocade, lapels and trousers.

81 Seix and Barral, *CC de luxe*
stage front, 63 × 44 cm, *c*1925

CHAPTER SIX

SPAIN AND EL TEATRO DE LOS NIÑOS

Seix and Barral of Barcelona

The history of the toy theatre in Spain is dominated by two Barcelona publishers, Seix and Barral and Paluzie. During the 1920s Seix and Barral published at least seven different stage fronts, as part of a children's theatre series patented by C.B. Nualart. A total of twenty-three plays were published, each of which had specially designed scenery and characters. Unlike other European toy theatres, the stage fronts often contained three-dimensional or moulded architectural features. However, the stage always remained the same size (28 × 16 cm) as did the backstage supports from which were hung the various scenes and backdrops.

A unique characteristic of the Seix and Barral scenes was the translucent backcloth. By applying different coloured tissue papers and illuminating it from behind, it was possible to create a variety of convincing lighting effects (Pl XXX).

Another peculiar characteristic of the theatres was the absence of a stage floor, so that the figures (operated on strips of card from the side or the rear) required an extra inch of card below their feet to bring them up to the height of the footlights in front (Fig 83). The major advantage of this system was that it did away with the need to use conspicuous operating wires, although it was necessary for the stage to be at eye level.

The plays were published in several languages, including English, and came with clear performance instructions written by Nualart:

The play should be read by the children, in the same manner as artists speak in the real theatre. They will also have to manipulate the actors. Once they are acquainted with the play the parts in the book should be cut by the printed lines. As these parts are numbered it will be sufficient for one child to have the even numbers and the other the [odd] numbers. Number 1 speaks . . . and number 2 gives his answer and so on.

THE DESIGNS

The largest and most elaborate of Seix and Barral's designs was the *CC de luxe* stage front, which came with ready-to-use scenery (Fig 81):

This model can be used for all scenes and plays published for the Children's Theatre and in its manufacture nothing that can add to its beauty has been spared. The effects that can be obtained and the durability of this model are well worth its price. All parts are finished and ready for use. There is nothing to be put together, and the children can start a play from the moment they have the theatre in their possession.

82 Seix and Barral (C.B.Nualart patent), *El Teatro de los Niños*, heading on a toy theatre sheet envelope, *c*1920

The other stage front produced by Seix and Barral was the smaller *BB* (Fig 84). Unlike the larger *CC* front, the proscenium and scenery had to be cut out and coloured tissue applied to the backcloth. Anticipating an audience for his youthful performers, Nualart even included entrance tickets with both these designs.

Seix and Barral's repertoire occupies a unique position in the field of European toy theatre. Although the plays were designed for performance on the Children's Theatre, their titles tended to be rather grown-up ones. There were historical dramas, two works by Shakespeare, an opera, as well as comedies of manners and cautionary tales. Artistically, the sets ranged from the impressionistic to the surrealistic. However, Mariano Bayon Alvarez, the Madrid architect and collector, has argued convincingly that most of the sets fall within the style of *Modernismo*, the Spanish art nouveau style that was radically altering the outlook of art and architecture at the time, and which found its clearest expression in the work of Antoni Gaudi.[1]

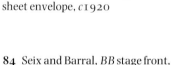

Paluzie

Long before Seix and Barral published their first toy theatres in the 1920s, another Barcelona publisher, Paluzie, had started producing more conventional stage fronts and character sheets.

In common with many of his European counterparts during the 1870s, Paluzie began his toy theatre career by producing sheets of figures in military and religious costume. The subjects of his works were far closer to the German, and particularly the north-eastern French, publishing houses. There were few complete plays and most of the scenery was of a generic nature, the only exceptions being a few Spanish locations: the bull ring, Puerto del Sol de Madrid and Pueblo. Stylistically, however, Paluzie remained close to his native Catalonia and today one finds far fewer of his theatres outside Spain than one does of Seix and Barral's. Much of Paluzie's work shows a keen awareness of the importance of Spanish theatrical history. His stage fronts often bear the names of great playwrights like Lope de Vega, Pedro Calderon de la Barca and Tirso de Molina, whose moral and social comedies profoundly influenced the development of European theatre (Pl XXXI).

83 Seix and Barral, detail of figure construction, from an original sheet envelope, *c*1920

84 Seix and Barral, *BB* stage front, *c*1925

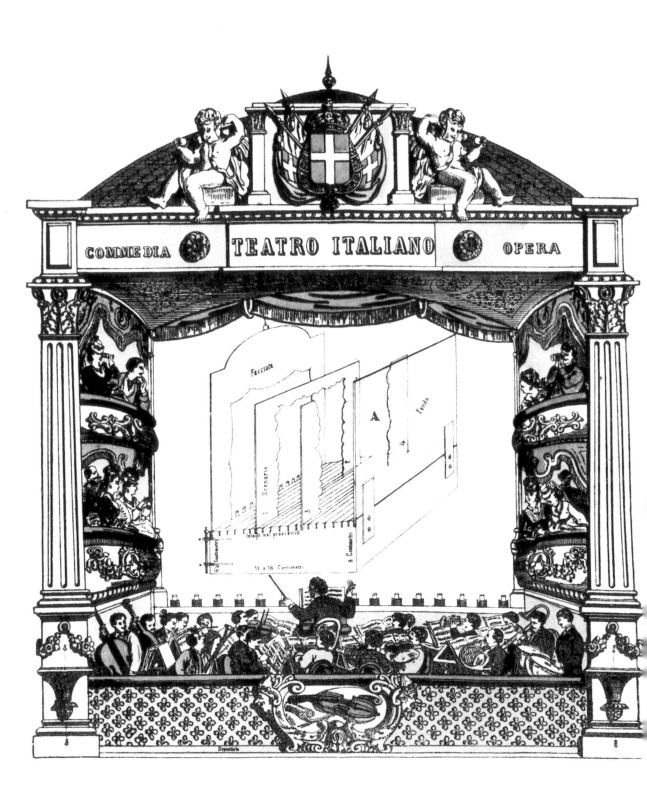

CHAPTER SEVEN

OTHER CONTINENTAL VARIATIONS

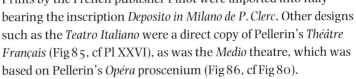

Teatro Italiano: Italy

Of the six or so Italian toy theatre publishers listed by Walter Röhler, all were based in Milan and all produced designs that were heavily influenced by the work of French publishers, especially Imagerie Pellerin of Epinal.

P. E. G. Vallardi of Milan produced his first toy theatre sheets between 1860 and 1870. These followed the French style of various generic scenes like forests and castles, rather than complete plays.

85 *Teatro Italiano*

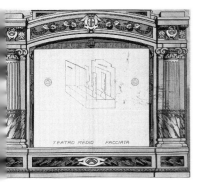

Prints by the French publisher Pinot were imported into Italy bearing the inscription *Deposito in Milano de P. Clerc*. Other designs such as the *Teatro Italiano* were a direct copy of Pellerin's *Théâtre Français* (Fig 85, cf Pl XXVI), as was the *Medio* theatre, which was based on Pellerin's *Opéra* proscenium (Fig 86, cf Fig 80).

86 *Teatro Medio*

Sweden and Norway

The proliferation of the toy theatre in Denmark was great enough to attract the interest of a few collectors and performers in Norway and Sweden where there was very little indigenous toy theatre. One of the few toy theatres to be produced in Norway was a Chinese-style one, published by C. Schibstedt of Oslo in 1963 (Fig 87).

★ ★

Holland

Although there are many toy theatre collectors and performers in
Holland, there are virtually no existing sheets, owing to an almost
total lack of indigenous toy theatre publishers. The stage front by
D. Bolle of Rotterdam in the collection of Ab Vissers, dates from
1860 and must be one of the only toy theatre sheets ever published
in Holland (Fig 88).

★ ★

Czechoslovakia

Incursions into the world of toy theatre in Czechoslovakia date
mostly from the beginning of this century. There are many extant
examples of large proscenia together with corresponding backcloths
and wings. However, there is very little information on publishers,
owing to an absence of printed names at the bottom of sheets.

87 C. Schibstedt, *Norwegian
Theatre*, 1963. The scene is from
Hans Christian Anderson's
The Emperor's Nightingale

Uitgave van A. Tjaden te Deventer.

88 D. Bolle, stage front, *c*1860

89 Scott and Co., Seltz's
American Boys' Theatre, drop-
curtain, *c*1870

TAIN.

CHAPTER EIGHT

NORTH AMERICA

★ ★ ★ ★ ★ ★ ★ ★ ★ ★ ★ ★ ★ ★ ★ ★ ★ ★ ★ ★

Outside Europe there was far less interest in the world of popular imagery and paper theatres, although George Speaight noted a 'manifestation of toy theatre in Japan . . . between 1750 and 1920 . . . a cut-out paper theatre . . . the *Kumitate-e*'.[1] This took the form of tableaux and scene sheets from the Kabuki drama but it was never intended to be performed on a detailed model stage. Occasionally the names of actors and theatres were added to the sheets: an exhibition of *Papiertheater* in Munich in 1977 included a number of figures representing actors at one of the Kabuki theatres in Tokyo at the end of the nineteenth century.

If the *Kumitate-e* ultimately drew its inspiration from the live stage, the same cannot be said, however, for the toy theatre in America. Here, the character and scene sheets that first began to appear during the last quarter of the nineteenth century were intended solely as toys for children and, as such, bore no relation to the live theatre. Publishers operating in New York and Boston tended to copy either English sheets, or produce adaptations of well-known fairy tales. It is possible that these were known as far afield as California, although available evidence does not suggest this, nor does it point to the existence of publishing sources either in Los Angeles or San Francisco.

★ ★ ★ ★ ★ ★ ★ ★ ★ ★ ★ ★ ★ ★ ★ ★ ★ ★ ★ ★

Scott and Co. and Seltz's *American Boys' Theatre*

The earliest known American toy theatre publisher is Scott and Co. of 146 Fulton Street, New York. From the early 1870s this firm began publishing toy theatre sheets under the imprint of Seltz's *American Boys' Theatre*. The first sheets warned the public against accepting worthless imitations:

The plays of Seltz's American Boys' Theatre are the only miniature theatricals ever published, giving full directions for working, etc. Every piece of the admirable series is put together and tested by professionals before being issued to the public. Pub. only by Scott and Co . . . where everything connected with the plays can be had, wholesale or retail. BE SURE AND ASK FOR AND TAKE NONE BUT SELTZ'S EDITION.

In spite of their verbosity, the claims of such advertisements have been unable to withstand the findings of recent research which suggest that the plays of the *American Boy's Theatre* were, in fact, direct copies of those published by the *Boys of England* magazine a few years earlier.

THE DESIGNS

In *Nineteenth Century Theatre Research*, George Speaight compared sheets for *King Arthur*, published in *Boys of England* with those that appeared in Seltz's *American Boys' Theatre*, under the title of *Sir Lancelot and Guinevere*.[2] Subsequent findings suggested that there was nothing inherently American about Scott and Co.'s sheets other

90 Edwin J. Brett, *Boys of England*, drop-curtain, 1868

than their titles. *Sir Lancelot and Guinevere* was virtually identical to *King Arthur*. Those differences that appeared were slight and were probably the result of Scott and Co. copying their sheets from *Boys of England* designs, rather than using the original wood-blocks.

Similar studies can be made of other of the Seltz plays. Around 1870 Scott and Co. published their version of a drop-curtain copied directly from *Boys of England* (Figs 89 and 90). Having established the existence of such piracy it is possible to construct a full list of plays which Scott and Co. cribbed and published under different titles:

Seltz's *American Boys' Theatre*	*Boys of England*
The Miller and His Men	*The Miller and His Men*
The Red Skeleton, or the Dead Avenger	*The Skeleton Horseman, or the Shadow of Death*
Redhead Jack, the Terror of London	*Jack Cade, or the Rebel of London*
The Boy Sailor, or the Pirate's Doom	*Tom Daring, or Far from Home*
The Fiend of the Rocky Mountains	*The Giant of the Black Mountains, or Jack and his eleven brothers*
The Pirates of the Florida Keys	*Alone in the Pirates' Lair*

In addition to the cribbed sheets, theatres were offered together with directions: 'I will commence at the beginning and tell you how to make your stage,' wrote the publisher, 'This, of course, may be made very elaborately, and a boy of a mechanical genius can easily improve on the following simple instruction.' Detailed measurements were provided; the proscenium was to be $11\frac{3}{4} \times 10''$, the stage $22 \times 11\frac{3}{4}''$. A wide range of accessories was also available, including gas lighting; footlights were a dollar, while rubber connecting tubes cost fifteen cents a foot.

Scott and Co. did not limit sales of their plays solely to New York. A number of their sheets bear the imprint of a retailer by the name of

BOYS' TOY THEATRES, 10 and 50 cts., 1 and 1 1-2 dollars, be sure to get one. TRIFET'S, 25 School St., Boston.

91 F. Trifet, retailer's card, *c*1870

Trifet at 25 School Street, Boston (Fig 91).[3] F. Trifet was in fact sole agent for Scott and Co. in the eastern United States.

★ ★

McLoughlin Brothers

In 1880, ten years after Scott and Co. started publishing their *American Boys' Theatre* sheets, another New York firm, McLoughlin Brothers, brought out its first design for a toy theatre. This was the work of John McLoughlin (b1827), a senior partner, who had been engraving and printing children's books, games and dolls' houses at 24 Beekman Street since 1855.

THE DESIGNS

McLoughlin Brothers published a number of different stage fronts, all of them with high-quality colour printing. Designs ranged from very basic, flat fronts to more elaborate designs like the *American Theatre* published in 1900 (Fig 92).

★ ★

J.H.Singer

On 15 May 1883, from his premises at 213 West 31st Street, New York, J.H.Singer patented his *Theatre Le Grand*. Singer seems to have published adaptations of existing plays to accompany his theatre. One of the first to appear was an abridged and adapted version of *The Miller and His Men*. Ironically, Singer omitted the most popular part of the play, the explosion and final destruction of the mill. The closing passage was thus rather tame in comparison:

Grindoff: Caught at last!

Karl: And in your own trap.

Kelmar: Lothair, Claudine is thine. Well dost thou deserve her.

(*curtain descends*)

92 McLoughlin Brothers, *American Theatre*, *c* 1900. The scene is from *Little Red Riding Hood*, one of the most popular of American toy theatre plays

Following *The Miller and His Men*, Singer advertised that the 'play of The Enchanted Lake [is] now ready. Price 1 dollar by mail, 15 cents extra for postage. The new play, The Last of the Mohicans will be ready April 1st 1885. Same price as The Enchanted Lake'.
Last of the Mohicans was one of the first plays inspired from American history to be adapted for the toy theatre.

Singer also employed an unusual system for operating his figures on the stage – the 'groove' system. The stage was constructed from strips of wood crossing from side to side. Scenery and figures were positioned inside the grooves that formed between the wooden strips. Lengths of cotton thread were tied to either side of their bases enabling them to be pulled across the stage. According to Singer, the best effects were achieved by moving the figures slowly.

★ ★

Other toy theatre publishers

Further piracy was perpetrated by Martin Studios of Willimantic, Connecticut. In 1916 this firm published *The Children's Play*, to

93 R. Schwarz, the *Imperial Theatre*, c1890. The scene is from *Little Red Riding Hood*

include *Cinderella, or the Magic Slipper* in five acts, each of seven tableaux. Both the text and stage designs were taken from a Danish production.

Other recorded American publishers include Richard Schwarz of New York, who published his *Imperial Theatre* stage front around 1890 (Fig 93), and Mark Salom of 333 Washington Street, Boston who sold toy theatres during the 1860s. These appeared in three sizes, with sheets of characters and scenery 5 × 3 inches and 10 × 12 inches. There is evidence that some of the characters may have been based upon contemporary Shakespearian actors on the New York stage.[4]

★ ★

Toy theatres in newspapers and magazines

Two newspapers are known to have regularly published character sheets in the pages of their art supplements. One was the *Baltimore Sunday Herald*, which published characters and scenery for a number of plays (Fig 94). Similar designs also appeared in the art supplement of the *Boston Sunday Globe*, together with printed stage fronts accompanied by the following instructions: 'the theatre is to be used in exhibiting the Boston Sunday Globe's series of historic tableaux, five in number, one tableaux [sic] each Sunday until completed.'

In 1918 further toy theatre sheets appeared in *The Delineator*, a magazine published from the Butterick Building in New York. It produced some very attractive designs, including a series for *The Wild Swans* (Fig 95), based on a tale by Hans Christian Anderson, together with another for *The Pied Piper of Hamelin*. Each series came with a well-written text and clear instructions on how to operate the characters. Magazines continued to include toy theatre sheets within their pages right into the 1930s. In 1933 *Child Life*, published by Rand McNally and Co. of Chicago, brought out its *Child Life Theatre*. With each year's subscription the reader received a free toy theatre and each month the magazine contained a page of characters and scenes to be cut out and glued together.

Numerous attempts to incorporate toy theatres into other products continued unabated up until the Second World War. In his book, *The Puppet Theatre in America*, Paul McPharlin mentions a product called *The Theatre Game* published by F. W. Woolworth.[5] This consisted of a stage ($7\frac{1}{2} \times 10''$), three scenes and figures for *Robin Hood*, *Little Red Riding Hood* and *Cinderella*. The aim was to shuffle numbers corresponding to numbers on each character and to read the parts of the character whose number one drew.

94 *Baltimore Sunday Herald*, figures for *Cinderella*, 9 February 1896

95 *The Delineator* Children's Theatre, *The Wild Swans*. 1918

THE DELINEATOR CHILDREN'S THEATER

The Wild Swans

Matinee for Children & scenery by McQuirn

The King

The Queen

The Brothers of Elise

Elise

Elise

Left Wing   Right Wing

Extra copies of this page, printed on heavy paper without lettering on the other side, may be obtained by sending five cents to the Picture Editor, care THE DELINEATOR, Butterick Building, New York.   Full directions for putting the theater together, and the complete text of the play appear on page 27 of this issue

CHAPTER NINE

THROUGH A CHILD'S EYES

One of the joys of studying toy theatres is to discover the great pleasure they have given adults. Nowhere is this more apparent than in the accounts of G. K. Chesterton, Robert Louis Stevenson and Charles Dickens. The importance of their writing lies in its ability to communicate, through a mixture of child-like vision and imagination, the essence of the toy theatre.

G. K. Chesterton and *George and the Dragon*

The origins of G. K. Chesterton's love of the toy theatre are best revealed in a passage from his autobiography of 1936:

The very first thing I can remember seeing with my own eyes was a young man walking across a bridge. He had a curly moustache and . . . carried in his hand a disproportionately large key of a shining yellow metal and wore a large golden crown. The bridge he was crossing sprang on the one side from the edge of a highly perilous mountain chasm, and at the other end it joined the upper part of the tower of an almost excessively castellated castle . . . To those who object that such a scene is rare in the home life of house agents living immediately to the North of Kensington High Street in the later seventies of the last century, I shall be compelled to admit, not that the scene was unreal, but that I saw it . . . through the proscenium of a toy theatre. . . . That one scene glows in my memory like a glimpse of some incredible paradise; and for all

96 G. K. Chesterton, the author at work on his toy theatre play *George and the Dragon*

145

I know I shall still remember it when all other memory is gone out of my mind.[1]

For Chesterton the toy theatre was far more than just a toy, it was a serious project, the importance of which he described in an article for the *Daily News*. This subsequently reappeared in a collection of essays entitled *Tremendous Trifles*:

There is only one reason why all grown-up people do not play with toys; and it is a fair reason. The reason is that playing with toys takes . . . much more time and trouble than anything else. Playing as children mean playing is the most serious thing in the world. . . . I have been myself attempting for some time past to complete a play in a small toy theatre that used to be called Penny Plain and Twopence Coloured; only that I drew and coloured the figures and scenes myself. . . . the play of St George and the Dragon over which I have burnt the midnight oil (you must colour the thing in by lamp-light because that is how it will be seen) still lacks, most conspicuously, alas, two wings of the Sultan's Palace , and also some comprehensible . . . way of getting up the curtain.[2]

The play Chesterton was attempting to produce, *George and the Dragon* (Figs 96, 97 and 98), was the subject of an article in *The Girl's Realm* in 1898:

The stage consisted of a very simple framework, with a drop curtain representing a sailing boat . . . The figures and scenes gave an immediate impression of character. It was important, Chesterton said, 'that the mere appearance of the dragon's head, if of proper ferocity, will be enough to explain that he intends to eat people . . . and that he has not merely dropped in to tea.'[3]

The story began in a witches palace, wherein that evil character informed the audience that, 'The King of Egypt has a daughter whom I have doomed to death and slaughter', her intention being that she will be eaten by the dragon. The monster's first appearance was made with seven different cut-out figures: the first very small, so as to appear tiny in the distance; the second larger as he crossed the moon from the other side of the stage; the third larger still, until the final one was so large that only its ferocious head could appear on the stage (Fig 97a).

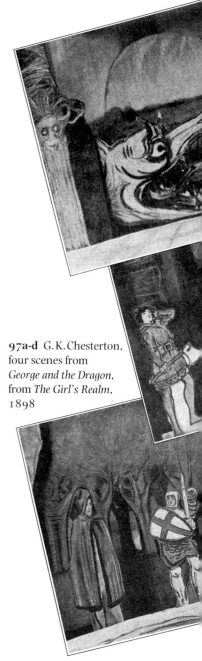

97a-d G. K. Chesterton, four scenes from *George and the Dragon*, from *The Girl's Realm*, 1898

97c George standing betwe[en] his uncle and Oberon

97a The dragon arrives

97b The three maidens arming George

Oberon, the fairy king, is at hand, ready to help George in his quest to fight the terrible dragon and rescue the fair princess. He summons three maidens who arm the hero with the weapons by which he can meet the foe on equal terms (Fig 97b), though the skill and courage to use them are left entirely to him (Fig 97c and d).

The result of the conflict is well-known: George is made a Saint and in Chesterton's final scene, the other six champions of Christendom arrive to join in the celebrations. The last tableau is of the slayer and his beloved standing above the head of the dead dragon (Fig 98).

Throughout his life Chesterton held firmly to the belief that toy theatres brought out the very best qualities in a human being. Speaking at the first exhibition of the Model Theatre Guild in 1925:

I had a primary tragedy at the age of two or three – it was that I could not get inside a theatre or onto the stage, where things happen immeasurably more interesting than in the real world. . . . To try and work up a whole performance on such a stage as this calls for very serious virtues of patience, endurance, resolution and so on. I come before you as a fraud – as one who has wasted his life in writing articles and things of that kind, whereas if I had lived up to the ideals of my childhood I might have produced the finest toy theatre in the world. . . . The things we do which are less worthy do not permit us to do the things which are really worth doing. Otherwise this kind of art would have risen to colossal proportions.[4]

97d The triumphs of St George

98 G. K. Chesterton, *George and the Dragon*, the defeat of the dragon, 1898

★ ★

Charles Dickens and *The Miller and His Men*

... we hear of a small theatre, with paint and red fire. ... It was
not an accident that Dickens ... loved it. It is a stage unsuited for
psychological realism; the cardboard characters cannot analyse
each other with any effect. But it is a stage almost divinely suited
for making surroundings, for making that situation and
background which belongs peculiarly to romance.
G. K. Chesterton on Dickens [5]

Like Chesterton, Dickens fell under the spell of toy theatres while he
was still a schoolboy. At Wellington House Academy he and his
friends 'mounted small theatres, and got up very gorgeous scenery
to illustrate The Miller and His Men. Dickens was always the leader
... Master Beverley constructed the Mill for us in such a way that it
could tumble to pieces with the assistance of crackers'. [6]

Between 1841 and 1842 Dickens built a toy theatre with assistance
from the stage designer Clarkson Stanfield RA, upon which he
performed a spectacular play:

This was called The Elephant of Siam and its production on a
proper scale of splendour necessitated the designing and painting of
several new scenes, which resulted in such competition between
my father and Stanfield that you would have thought that their
very existence depended on the mounting of this same elephant.
And even after Stanfield had had enough of it, my father was still
hard at work and pegged away at the landscapes and architecture
... with an amount of energy which in any other man would have
been extraordinary, but which I soon learned to look upon as quite
natural in him. [7]

XXIX *Journal Des Petites Filles,*
Théâtre De La Poupée Modèle, c1870

XXX Seix and Barral, toy
theatre, *c*1920. The scene is of the
Bridge of Sighs from *The Merchant
of Venice*

XXXI Paluzie, stage front, *c*1900

LOPE CALDERÓN TIRSO

D. Diego Tenorio.   D.ª Inés.   D. Juan Tenorio.

★ ★

Robert Louis Stevenson and *A Penny Plain and Twopence Coloured*

Perhaps the most enduring of all writings on the toy theatre are those of Robert Louis Stevenson, the author of an essay published in *The Magazine of Art* in 1884, entitled *A Penny Plain and Twopence Coloured*. Stevenson's interest in the toy theatre began when he was a child living in Edinburgh. Here, he would often pass 'a certain stationer's shop' at the corner of the main road that connected Edinburgh with Leith:

XXXII J. Redington, the *Neptune Theatre*, c1870

When, upon any Saturday, we made a party to behold the ships, we passed that corner; and since in those days, I loved a ship as a man loves Burgundy or daybreak, this of itself had been enough to hallow it. But there was more than that. In the Leith Walk window . . . there stood displayed a theatre in working order, with a 'forest set' . . . and a few 'robbers carousing' in the slides; and below and about, dearer tenfold to me the plays themselves, those budgets of romance . . . and then to go within . . . and, closely watched, be suffered to undo those bundles and breathlessly devour those pages of gesticulating villains . . . it was a giddy joy . . . every sheet we fingered was another lightning glance into obscure, delicious story . . . The crux of Buridan's donkey was as nothing to the uncertainty of the boy as he handled and doated on these bundles of delight . . . and the boy was forth again . . . the lamps springing into light in the blue winter's even, and The Miller, or The Rover . . . clutched against his side . . . how he laughed aloud in exultation! I can hear that laughter still.[8]

Here then lay the source of the toy theatre's attraction to Stevenson: the intense emotion experienced in handling those 'bundles of delight' and the manner in which they played on his childish sensibilities: 'The purchase and the first half hour at home, that was the summit. Thenceforth the interest declined little by little. The fable as set forth in the play-book, proved to be not worthy of the scenes and characters'.[9] However, the physical joy of preparing and colouring in the character and scene sheets always remained:

With crimson lake (crimson lake! – the horns of elfland are not richer on the ear) . . . and Prussian blue a certain purple is to be compounded which, for cloaks especially, Titian could not equal. . . . But when all was painted, it is needless to deny it, all was spoiled. You might, indeed, set up a scene or two to look at; but to cut the figures out was simply sacrilege; nor could any child twice court the tedium, the worry, and the long drawn disenchantment of an actual performance.[10]

★ ★

Toy theatres and the Victorian novel

Yet interest in the delights of toy theatres went beyond mere evocations of childhood emotion; they became an integral part of the stories of many of the most famous novels published during the nineteenth century.

In *Vanity Fair* William Makepeace Thackeray describes the visit of two young men, Master George Osborne and Master Todd, to 'all the principal theatres of the metropolis'. Both these characters 'knew all the actors from Drury Lane to Sadlers Wells; and performed, indeed, many of the plays to the Todd family and their youthful friends, with West's famous characters, on their pasteboard theatre'.[11]

Thomas Mann, in his epic story of the Buddenbrooks family, describes a scene in which Hanno, the young son, anxiously awaits the moment on Christmas night when the great doors will be flung open to reveal the tree and all the presents below:

The whole great room was filled with the fragrance of slightly singed evergreen twigs and glowing with light from countless tiny flames. . . . Hanno was quite dazed. His fevered glance had soon sought out the theatre, which, as it stood there upon the table, seemed larger and grander than anything he had dared to dream of. . . . Ah, here was the prompter's box, a shell shaped one, and a beautiful red and gold curtain rolled up and down behind it. The stage was set for the first act of Fidelio. The poor prisoners stood with folded hands. Don Pizarro, in enormous puffed sleeves, was

99 J. Yeats, characters for
James Flaunty

striking a permanent and awsome attitude, and the minister, in black velvet, approached from behind with hasty strides to turn all to happiness.[12]

The theatre being described in this scene might well have been one by Joseph Scholz of Mainz, particularly in view of the shell-shaped prompter's box (cf Pl XV), and the fact that Scholz included *Fidelio* in its list of plays.

Not all Victorian writers were content to let the toy theatre feature merely as a component of their novels. The playwright and artist Jack Yeats, brother of W. B. Yeats, occupied long hours of his time preparing text and characters for entire plays (Fig 99). These were later praised in an article written for *The Mask* by Edward Gordon Craig: 'His dramas are filled with all the winds of Heaven. They are short . . . yet no-one who reads them but feels they are as long as life . . . not one word too many nor too few, and it isn't as though the cackle had been cut for the mere 'osses . . . it's cut for the human soul'.[13]

Yeats's own descriptions of these events were less verbose and decidedly more practical:

Seeing that to make a play go without a hitch the *business* must be very simple, I write all my plays with as little movement for the figures as possible . . . though . . . I have some characters of whose *business* I am very proud. . . . there was a town crier who moved his arm and rang his bell, and a clown who smoked a pipe with real smoke.[14]

For all its ability to evoke childhood memories and feelings, the toy theatre was, quite simply, an object of profound beauty. For many of these writers it was an art form in its own right:

The most artistic thing about theatrical art is the fact that the spectator looks at the whole thing through a window. . . . the advantage of the small theatre is that you are looking through a small window. Has not everyone noticed how sweet and startling any landscape looks when seen through an arch. This strong, square shape, this shutting off of everything else, is not only an assistance to beauty; it is the essential of beauty.[15]

Pollock, Webb, Diaghilev and *The Triumph of Neptune*

In 1926 the Russian impressario, Serge Diaghilev, was looking for a new, typically English theme as the subject of a ballet to be danced by his travelling company, the Ballet Russes. At a loss for ideas, he consulted the writer and poet Sacheverell Sitwell, who offered a number of suggestions, none of which Diaghilev found acceptable. Finally, in a state of desperation Diaghilev visited the shops of Benjamin Pollock in Hoxton and H. J. Webb in Old Street. Here, he found inspiration in the form of hundreds of dusty sheets depicting characters and scenery from the plays and pantomimes of the Victorian age.

Together with Sitwell, Diaghilev spent several days going through the old sheets and finally selected some fifty-eight different prints, which he was given permission to adapt as he wished. Sitwell set to work on constructing a plot around the visual schemes suggested by the sheets, while Lord Berners was commissioned to compose the music for the score. *The Triumph of Neptune (or an English Pantomime in twelve tableaux)* received its world première at the Lyceum in London on 3 December 1926. It is the only recorded instance of a live stage production to be adapted from the miniature plays of the toy theatre.

Discovering precisely which sheets were used by the designer, Prince Alexander Schervashidze, and the costume designer, Pedro Pruna, is extremely difficult. There are very few extant photographs of the ballet; those that do survive are publicity shots taken against only two backcloths, rather than detailed production photographs. Study of Sitwell's original notebook and scenario of the ballet does, however, shed some light on the derivation of most of the other sheets used in the production.[1] Other sources of information include notes from the original 1926 programme and photographs of a number of sheets that came up for auction at Sotheby's, London in May 1984, as well as contemporary reviews in newspapers and magazines. These praise the splendour of the giant-size, twopenny coloured sets, but provide few other details.

Let us therefore study the ballet's scenes in the order in which they appear in the original programme:

ACT I

Scene 1. London Bridge

The first scene was almost certainly
based on Scene 2, No 2 of John
Redington's *Paul Clifford* (Fig 100),
as specified by Sitwell in his
notebook. In the ballet, a crowd of
Londoners gather round a magic
telescope, through which the fairy
realm can be observed. A journalist
and a sailor of the Royal Navy are
about to make an exploration into
the fairy world.

100 J.Redington, *Paul Clifford*,
Scene 2, No 2

Scene 2. Cloudland

For this tableau Sitwell suggested
either Redington's *Timour the
Tartar* (Scene 1, No 2), or Pollock's
New Sky scene, both of which
would have been suitable.
However, a later entry in Sitwell's
notebook specifies *Timour the
Tartar*. The text describes the
inhabitants of Cloudland
disporting themselves amid the
clouds. Sitwell proposed an
ensemble of dancing fairies, sprites
and harlequins.

Scene 3. Farewell

The explorers are seen bidding
goodbye to their loved ones
(Fig 101). Sitwell's notes say no
more than the sailor and a girl sit
on a bench outside a house in the
moonlight. The set was possibly
based on one of the many
pantomime harlequinade street
scenes, any one of which could
have easily been adapted.

101 *The Triumph of Neptune*, Act I,
Scene 3, *Farewell*, the explorers set off
for Cloudland. A publicity photograph
with Lord Berners, the composer,
between the sailor and his sweetheart

Scene 4. Shipwreck

No sooner have the explorers set
sail than Neptune asserts his
powers and they are shipwrecked.
For this tableau Sitwell specified
the backscene from Pollock's *The
Blind Boy* (Scene 4, No 5), with its
sublime rocks, crashing waves and
forked lightning (Fig 102).

102 B.Pollock, *The Blind Boy*,
Scene 4, No 5

Scene 5. Fleet Street

Back in London two rival
newspapers – the *Evening Telescope*
and the *Evening Microscope* –
compete for the scoop of the
explorers' voyage. This was
undoubtedly set before a
pantomime harlequinade street
scene usually portraying two shops
or offices in a London street. This
tableau was not indicated in
Sitwell's notes and was probably
added at a later date to cover the
considerable change between
Scenes 4 and 6.

Scene 6. The Frozen Wood

In this scene – 'a magic forest
glistening with snow and
moonlight' – Sitwell proposed that
the Fairy Queen and her attendants
welcome the sailor and the
journalist (Fig 103). A fanfare is
heard attracting the attention of
the explorers. The Fairy Queen
attempts to dissuade them but they
insist on finding the source of the
sound. The backcloth for this

103 *The Triumph of Neptune*, Act I, Scene 6, *The Frozen Wood*, the Fairy Queen's attendants welcome the explorers

tableau (Fig 103) is clearly that in Scene 4, No 4 of Pollock's *Sleeping Beauty* (Fig 104). Sitwell also made effective use of the flying ballet, in which dancers, connected by floral garlands, travelled through the air 'to form lovely and ever changing designs'.

104 B. Pollock, *The Sleeping Beauty*, Scene 4, No 4

ACT II

Scene 1. Dance of the Goddess
This was a solo scene, specially choreographed by Georges Balanchine for the dancer, Sokolova. There is no indication in Sitwell's notes about the source of the drop-curtain, but it may well have been one of the fine act drops published by H. J. Webb (Fig 105).

105 H. J. Webb, *New Fairy Scene*, front scene

Scene 2. The Giant Hand
The programme states that the scene is a corner of London, near the absent sailor's home. A dandy is making advances to his wife, and to display his Terpsichorean talents, dances a polka to the strains of a nearby brass band. They go indoors where 'strange things are happening behind the blinds of an illuminated window'. Sensing something is amiss, the spirit of the sailor returns to see his wife in the dandy's arms. He lifts a

knife to attack the dandy but is spotted by two policeman who try to overpower him (Fig 106). But he is no more than an empty shadow and he returns to fairyland.

106 *The Triumph of Neptune*, Act II, Scene 2, *The Giant Hand*. This is probably a publicity shot staged before the backcloth from Act II, Scene 5

Sitwell used Scene 11, No 11 from Pollock's *Sleeping Beauty* for one of the known backcloths for this scene. This was a pantomime street scene of a window containing a large hand holding a quill. However it is possible that Scene 18 of Pollock's *Oliver Twist* might also have been used.

Scene 3. The Ogre's Castle
Back in fairyland we now find the explorers in the Ogre's castle. For this tableau Sitwell used Pollock's *Sleeping Beauty*. Having initially employed an exterior scene, in which the explorers listened to a poem recited through

a mask, Sitwell finally decided on an interior scene (Fig 107). Here, the journalist was seized by the Ogre's satellites and sawn in half.

107 B. Pollock, *The Sleeping Beauty*, Scene 1, No 1

Scene 4. Sunday Morning in London

The story continues with a drunken Negro (danced by Balanchine himself) managing to break the magic telescope, thus severing all contact between earth and the fairy world. Although this might indicate a return to the opening *London Bridge* scene, it is more likely that a further scene change was envisaged. Sitwell's notes repeatedly list *London Scene* or *Nigger and Telescope* with Pollock's name alongside. A likely contender may have been Scene 6, No 6 – a street scene – from Pollock's *Oliver Twist*, and a photograph in the Sotheby's sale showed this particular sheet squared off prior to enlargement.

Scene 5. The Triumph of Neptune

Abandoned by his wife on earth, the sailor accepts fairy form and, transformed into a fairy prince, he weds Neptune's daughter. Fortunately the design for the backcloth of this scene survives in the form of an original photograph (Fig 108).

108 *The Triumph of Neptune*, Act II, Scene 5

This shows a cut-out version of Scene 1 from Pollock's *Silver Palace* (Fig 109), backed by Scene 3, No 3 from Webb's *Jack and the Beanstalk* (Fig 110).

109 B. Pollock, *The Silver Palace*, Scene 1, No 1

110 H. J. Webb, *Harlequin Jack and the Beanstalk*, Scene 3, No 3

Scene 6. Apotheosis

The final scene featured the unexpected transformation of the sailor into a fairy prince, possibly inspired from a similar scene in Pollock's *Sleeping Beauty*.

It seems extraordinary that one cannot be more specific about the design of the ballet, and that there are not more contemporary photographs taken in front of a greater variety of backcloths. Naturally the critics concentrated on the quality of the dance, but it would be fascinating to discover more about the Juvenile Drama's involvement in this most Victorian of Russian ballets.

APPENDIX II

Basic

structures of

toy theatres

The early nineteenth-century wooden stage

The Regency and early Victorian theatre was a modest affair: a wooden stage, four wooden uprights and spreaders and a series of crossbars to hold the scenery in place (Fig 111). Applied to the front of this structure was a printed, paper proscenium, usually hand-coloured and strengthened with cardboard. Below this would be the orchestra strip. A curtain of linen or paper would be inserted at the appropriate place behind the stage opening.

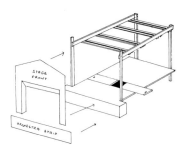

111 Basic structure of a Regency wooden theatre

Many English stages incorporated a trapdoor of the 'grave' type (two sliding panels in the centre of the stage), a design still common to many reproductions sold today by Pollock's Toy Museum. Some of William West's more elaborate models were also built with traps of the 'rise and sink' variety, a system most commonly used in Denmark.

To be used flat or built

From the very beginning most English publishers printed their stage fronts on sheets of paper or card, to be cut out in such a way as to create a three-dimensional effect and the illusion of depth (Fig 112).

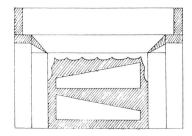

112 Line drawing indicating how, by cutting away the shaded areas and folding accordingly, a recessed arch can be produced

There was tremendous scope for creating elaborate designs on these basic fronts. They usually featured at least two stage boxes above stage doors, one either side of the proscenium arch, housing a variety of bewhiskered gentlemen, and ladies with ringlets.

Auditorium lighting, in the form of lamps with opaque glass globes and pendant lustres, was often included either side of the stage. Much of the designer's imagination was, however, reserved for the pediment above the proscenium arch. Very often this would contain representations of gods or legendary figures, such as Britannia, Mars, Apollo and Neptune. There might also be angels or cherubim frolicking in chariots, either side of a royal coat of arms, and a bust of Shakespeare.

To some extent these designs were based on those in the live theatre. Some stage fronts were certainly direct copies of famous theatres like Drury Lane and Covent Garden. The important thing to remember is that most of these early stages reflect the period in which they were built (approx 1811-50), and it is this quality which is of paramount importance in judging the beauty of a piece today.

Very few proscenia produced on the Continent followed the English-style, recessed-arch design. European theatres were generally grander and more elegant than their English counterparts. Designed in the classical style, they often incorporated statuesque figures in niches, either side of the arch. Rarely did they have boxes or audience, nor did they have an orchestra strip.

Papiertheater in Germany

In Germany the standard toy theatre design was established by J.F.Schreiber's publication in 1886 of Hugo Elm's *Das Kindertheater*. This contained an illustration of the back of a stage and the perspective arrangement of wing-pieces. These were slotted into the stage floor and had designs on both sides to allow for rapid scene changes (Fig 113).

113 The basic format of the German papiertheater, as illustrated by Hugo Elm in 1886

The stage itself was a large box which, when packed, contained all the necessary components for one play including proscenium (in three sections), backdrops, wing-pieces and figures.

The Danish Dukketeater

In 1880 Alfred Jacobsen designed a miniature stage which has remained the standard format for Danish toy theatres. The stage was large and fronted by a flat, neo-classical proscenium, based on the Royal Theatre in Copenhagen. It even carried the same motto over the proscenium arch – *Ei Blot Til Lyst* ('Not only for pleasure') – as a permanent reminder to the young stage manager. Like the German model, there were no slats across the top to hold the scenery; instead wing pieces and backdrops were clipped into free-standing supports (Fig 114). The height of the stage also allowed scenery to be 'flown', that is, to be attached to crossbars, which in turn could be raised

above the proscenium arch (Fig 114). There were usually two trapdoors in the stage floor; the centre stage contained a trap which could be raised and lowered by a pulley system, while at the back there was a simpler, 'grave' trap.

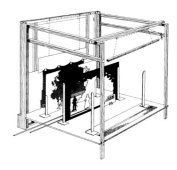

114 Basic structure of a Danish toy theatre

Danish toy theatres developed into incredibly complex pieces of equipment. The *Illustrated Family Journal* regularly published theatre designs which required the reader to provide their own wood and cardboard structure. Each model incorporated a new and unique feature such as a moving belt system for operating characters on the stage, a mechanism for flying scenery and a shadow play.

Théâtre Français

A number of different stage fronts were published in France. These were mostly produced by Pellerin, which still operates from buildings on the banks of the Moselle. Their *Théâtre Français* incorporated an innovative system of grooves in the stage floor, into which scenes and characters could be inserted. A series of pictorial instructions printed at the bottom of each design, showed how these could allow for quick scene changes (Fig 115).

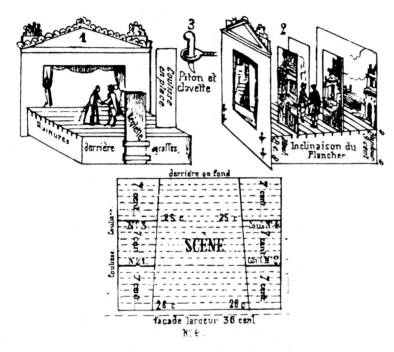

115 Building instructions printed by Pellerin on their stage fronts and scene sheets

Spain – *El Teatro de los Niños*

The Spanish toy theatre was entirely the product of two Barcelona firms, Paluzie and Seix and Barral, who produced designs by C.B. Nualart. In spite of a variety of elegant and elaborate stage fronts, the basic backstage structure of Nualart's theatres remained the same, as did the size of the scenery (21 × 30 cm) (Fig 116).

116 Backstage construction of a Nualart theatre

Home-made theatres

The examples of stages listed above, could all be bought ready-made and coloured and required a minimum of effort to put them together. While some were larger and more complex than others, they shared a common objective: they were a means of recreating in miniature, the lively and colourful world of the stage. However, if the cost of a manufactured theatre proved prohibitive, a little imagination could easily transform a wooden packing-case or cardboard box into the perfect miniature stage (Fig 117).

117 A simple home-made 'box' theatre

By the simple expedient of upturning the box and cutting a hole at the front for the proscenium, two holes – one on each side – through which to operate the figures and a series of slits at the top to support the scenery, a complete theatre was created. A simple design painted on the proscenium arch, home-made characters and sets and the performance could begin.

Notes

INTRODUCTION

1 Peter Winn, *Plays by British publishers represented in the Sage Collection* (unpublished dissertation, University of Victoria, British Columbia, 1975)

2 Sybil Rosenfeld, 'Sadlers Wells Scene Book', *Theatre Notebook*, 15, pp 57-62

3 *Drury Lane Scenes; a secondary record*, exh cat, Tyne and Wear County Council Museum, 1979, pp 60-63

4 George Speaight, *Juvenile Drama. The history of the English Toy Theatre* (London, 1946), 2nd edn published as *Toy Theatre* (London, 1969).

5 Ellen Terry, *The Mask*, V (Florence, 1912-13), p 3. *The Mask* was a quarterly journal on the art of the theatre, published privately by Edward Gordon Craig from Arena Goldoni, Florence

6 Edward Gordon Craig, 'Prologue', *The Mask*, V (Florence, 1912-13), pp 1-2

CHAPTER ONE

1 Henry Mayhew, interview with West, *Morning Chronicle*, 25 February 1850. These lines are from the pantomime *Harlequin and Mother Goose or the Golden Egg*, first performed at Covent Garden Theatre on 29 December 1806 with Joe Grimaldi as the clown. 'Bang-up' was slang for the height of style or fashion. In the pantomime Grimaldi transformed a cradle, four cheeses and a fender into a small coach drawn by a dog, satirizing the notorious eccentric, Romeo Coates

2 Matthew Skelt was the founder of this long-established family firm which specialized in publishing toy theatre sheets at Swan Street, Minories in the City between 1835 and 1872

3 A. Park was another publisher who produced toy theatre sheets between 1818 and 1880 from a number of addresses in London including 47 Leonard St, Finsbury, 40 Marshall St, 150 High Street, Notting Hill and 30 St John's Road, Hoxton

4 The original production of *Harlequin Old Dame Trot* took place at the Surrey Theatre in 1837

5 The original production of the *Wood Daemon* was at the Lyceum Theatre in 1811. Skelt probably reprinted earlier sheets by Robert Lloyd. Rhoderick Dhu was a character in an unidentified play.

6 A. E. Wilson, *Penny Plain, Twopence Coloured* (London, 1932), pp 29-31 and George Speaight, *op cit* (1969), pp 34-9

7 Peter Winn, *op cit*

8 Until George Speaight's discovery of Mayhew's interview with William West (cf note 1) it was never considered that J. H. Jameson was a woman. Although Mayhew was reticent about giving full names, he quotes West as saying, 'Mrs J –, who lived at Dukes Court, Bow St . . . sold my prints at first and then she began to print and publish for herself.' George Speaight and Gerald Morice discovered the existence of the article when it was republished in the Pelican edition of *The Unknown Mayhew*, from the original piece in the *Morning Chronicle*, 25 February 1850

9 Twelfth Night characters evolved from ancient customs as part of that day's celebrations. A sheet was divided into twenty-four sections, each containing a caricature with such names as Lucretia Lovely, Delia Do-it-All and Toby Tipple. These were cut out and drawn from a hat, each person playing the character drawn.

10 H. S. Marks RA, *Pen and Pencil Sketches*, vol 2 (1894), pp 6-15

11 George Speaight, 'Notes and Queries', *Theatre Notebook*, XLI, no 3 (1987), p 140

12 *Zoroaster* was written by W. T. Moncrieff, and received its first performance at the Theatre Royal, Drury Lane in 1824

13 Robert Louis Stevenson, 'A Penny Plain and Twopence Coloured', in *Memories and Portraits*, Chatto & Windus edn (London, 1920), pp 131-9. This essay was originally published in April 1884 in *The Magazine of Art* and subsequently republished in a series of essays entitled *Memories and Portraits* (London, 1887)

14 Ralph Thomas, *Notes and Queries*, IV (27 August 1898), p 164. This was originally issued on a weekly basis from its inception in November 1849, becoming monthly in 1953. It acted as a forum for debate for readers, writers, collectors and librarians and included correspondance on toy theatre matters

15 Robert Lloyd, published toy theatre sheets between 1828 and 1833 at 40 Gibson Street, opposite the Coburg Theatre (now the Old Vic).

16 H. E. Frances-Eagle, 'The Webb Juvenile Drama', *The Mask*, V (Florence, 1912-13), p 347

17 Robert Louis Stevenson, *op cit* (1920), p 131-9

18 A. E. Wilson, *op cit*, p 72

19 John Redington (1819-76), published toy theatre sheets between 1850 and 1876 at 208 Hoxton Old Town (renumbered 73 Hoxton Street)

20 Benjamin Pollock (1856-1937), published toy theatre sheets between 1876 and 1937, whereupon the business was managed by his daughters Selina and Louisa until 1944

21 Barry Clarke, 'Note', *Theatre Notebook*, XXVIII, no 3, p 139

22 A copy of the marriage certificate is in the author's collection. Sadly, Eliza died at an early age leaving Benjamin to look after their children as well as the shop.

23 George Speaight, *op cit* (1969), p75. This was in fact a later reminiscence by one of B.Pollock's daughters, but provided no indication of Toft's background, nor how long he worked for Pollock

24 Newspaper interview of 21 December 1930

25 Letter in the collection of George Speaight

26 Ditto

27 H.C.Sage's collection was bought by the University of Victoria, British Columbia in 1963, and was the subject of an unpublished dissertation by Peter Winn (cf INTRODUCTION, note 1)

28 Conversation with Conetta's daughter (St Helier, Jersey 1984)

29 George Skelt (*alias* Conetta), 'The Model Stage, or the Juvenile Drama', *The Puppet Master – Journal of the British Puppet and Model Theatre Guild* (January 1955). The British Puppet and Model Theatre Guild was originally founded in 1925 as the British Model Theatre Guild, changing its name in 1932

30 Robert Louis Stevenson, *op cit* (1920), pp131-9

31 Information on this firm was provided by a former employee, during a radio phone-in with the author in Nottingham in 1985. He clearly recalled the time in 1914 when, at the age of fourteen, he was working for Joseph Johnson, or 'Holy Joe', as he was known: 'He would appear from nowhere, wearing a smoking jacket and keeping a weather eye on his workers'. The employee also remembered whole trees arriving at the works to be cut up and whittled down into tops, whips, draught pieces and skipping-rope handles.

32 Gamages catalogue (1906). Reprinted by Denys Ingram (1982)

CHAPTER TWO

1 F.N.Campe, published toy theatre sheets in Nuremberg *c*1840

2 Walter Röhler, *Grosse Liebe Zu Kleinen Theatern* (Hamburg, 1963)

3 Most of the information on Theodor Guggenberger was provided by his son Ralph, who lived in Munich until his own death in 1978. Some years earlier, Bavarian television made a film about Theodor Guggenberger, some of it shot in a house in St John's Wood using the theatre of Dr Kurt Pfluger with scenes from plays incorporating Guggenberger's designs. Much of the information on J.F.Schreiber came from the scholarly monograph, *Schreiber's Kinder Theater*, written by Pfluger and Helmut Herbst, published in 1986

4 Letter from Dr Kurt Pfluger to the author (1984)

CHAPTER THREE

1 George Garde, *Theater Geschichte Im Spiegel Der Kindertheater* ('The Theatre as reflected in the Toy Theatre') (Copenhagen, 1971)

2 Letter from National Museum, Copenhagen to the author (1984)

CHAPTER FIVE

1 Walter Röhler, *op cit*, p37

CHAPTER SIX

1 Mariano Bayon Alvarez, *Arquetecturas di Papel*, exh cat, Madrid, 1980

CHAPTER EIGHT

1 George Speaight, introduction to *Papier Theater*, exh cat, Puppentheatersammlung, Stadt Museum, Munich, 1977

2 George Speaight, 'Was there ever an American Toy Theatre', *Nineteenth Century Theatre Research*, I (Autumn 1973)

3 From the personal collection of Christopher Williams

4 Paul McPharlin, *The Puppet Theatre in America*, 2nd edn (Boston, 1969), ch XVII, p313

5 *Ibid.*

CHAPTER NINE

1 G.K.Chesterton, *Autobiography* (London, 1936), ch 2, pp31-2

2 G.K.Chesterton, 'The Toy Theatre', in *Tremendous Trifles* (London, 1909)

3 George Knollys, 'Mr Gilbert Chesterton and His Toy Theatre', article in *The Girl's Realm*, 9 (1898), pp617-23

4 Newspaper report on the opening of the British Model Theatre Guild's exhibition at the Faculty of Arts Gallery by G.K.Chesterton, *Daily Telegraph* (25 August 1925) and the *Manchester Guardian* of the same date

5 G.K.Chesterton, 'The Youth of Dickens', *Biography of Charles Dickens* (London, 1906)

6 Article by Charles Culliford Boz Dickens, *Daily News* (15 May 1895)

7 *Ibid.*

8 Robert Louis Stevenson, *op cit* (1920), pp131-9

9 *Ibid.*

10 *Ibid.*

11 George Speaight, *op cit* (1969), p98

12 Thomas Mann, *Buddenbrooks*, 2nd English edn (London, 1947), p434

13 Allen Carric (*alias* Edward Gordon Craig), '"Captain Jack B. Yeats". A Pirate of the Old School', *The Mask*, V (Florence, 1912-13), p44

14 Robin Skelton (ed), *The Collected Plays of Jack B. Yeats*, (London, 1971), pp17-19

15 G.K.Chesterton, *op cit* (1909)

APPENDIX I

1 The original notebook is contained in the Harry Ransom Humanities Research Centre, University of Texas at Austin under, Works 20, *The Triumph of Neptune*, AMS with few emendations (1926), scenario for ballet

Chronological list of toy theatre publishers

The following information is gratefully extracted from George Speaight's comprehensive listing in *Juvenile Drama* (1946) and *Toy Theatre* (1969).

1811-54

William West
· 13 Exeter St, later
· 57 Wych St, Strand

1811-14 and 1832-60

I. K. Green
· Clements Inn Passage, Clare Market
· 3 George St, Walworth
· 33 Salisbury Place, Walworth
· 34 Lambeth Square, New Cut
· 16 Park Place, Walworth
· 9 Thurlow Place, Walworth

1811-14

Mrs M. Hebberd
· 2 Upper Charlton St, Fitzroy Square, Marylebone

1811-27

Mrs J. H. Jameson
· 13 Dukes Court, Bow St

1812

H. Burtenshaw
· 130 St Martin's Lane

1812-24

W. Love
· 81 Bunhill Row, Finsbury

1818-80

A. Park (in partnership with J. Goulding)
· 6 Old St Road
· 6 Oakley St, Lambeth
  succeeded by:

Archibald Park (*c*1835-63)
· 47 Leonard St, Finsbury

Sarah Park (*c*1863-67)
· 47 Leonard St, Finsbury

Alexander Park (*c*1867-80)
· 47 Leonard St, Finsbury
  then
· 40 Marshall St
· 150 High St, Notting Hill
· 30 St John's Rd, Hoxton

1821-24

W. Clarke
· 265 High Holborn

1822-30

Hodgson and Co.
· 43 Holywell St
· 11 King St, Snow Hill
· 10 Newgate St
· 111 Fleet St
· 10 Cloth Fair, W Smithfield

1822-39

J. L. Marks
· 17 Artillery St, Bishopsgate
· 23 Russell Court, Drury Lane
· 91 Long Lane, Smithfield
· 6 Worship St, Finsbury Square

1822

J. Allen
· 23 Princes Rd, Kennington

1824-28

F. Edwards
· 49 Leman St, Goodman's Fields

1825-30

D. Straker
· 21 Aldersgate St

1827-31

Dyer
· 13 Dorset Cres, Hoxton New Town
· 55/33 Bath St, City Road
· Featherstone Buildings, City Road
· 109 Aldersgate St

1828-33

Robert Lloyd
· 40 Gibson St (opposite the Coburg Theatre, now the Old Vic)

1830

J. Bailey and Co.
· 1 Clifford's Inn Passage
· 13 Fetter Lane
· 65 Grays Inn Lane, Holborn
· 2 Slades Place, Little Suffolk St
· 188 Fleet St

1831-43

Orlando Hodgson
· 10 Cloth Fair, W Smithfield
· 22 Macclesfield St
· 111/118/132 Fleet St

1832

Sarah Stokes
· 57 Wych St, Strand

1835-72

Skelt family
M. Skelt (1835-*c*1837)
M. & M. Skelt (*c*1837-40)
M. & B. Skelt (1840-50)
B. Skelt (1850-62)
E. Skelt (1862-72)
· 17 Swan St, Minories

1844-1933

W. Webb (1844-90) succeeded by:
H. J. Webb (1890-1933)

· Ripley, Surrey
· Cloth Fair, Bermondsey
· 49/104/124/146 Old St, St Luke's

1850-76

John Redington
· 208 Hoxton Old Town (renumbered 73 Hoxton St)

1876-1944

Benjamin Pollock (1876-1937) succeeded by his daughters **Selina and Louisa** (1937-44)
· 73 Hoxton St, Hoxton

1886-1906

A. How Mathews
· Churchfield Rd, Acton

1899-1956

G. Skelt (*alias* G. Conetta, born G. Wood)
· 24 Clairview St, St Helier, Jersey

1946-52

Benjamin Pollock Ltd
· 1 John Adam St, Adelphi
· 16 Little Russell St

1955-69

Pollock's Toy Museum
· 44 Monmouth St

1969-

Pollock's Toy Museum/ Pollock's Toy Theatres Ltd
· 1 Scala St

PENNY PACKET PUBLISHERS

Here we find the only signs of toy theatre publishing outside London.

c1870

Bishop and Co.
· Houndsditch

1875-c1900

H. G. Clarke
· 2 Garrick St, Covent Garden
· 252 Strand

c1880

J. Gage
· Pembroke Place, Liverpool

S. Marks and Sons
(successors to Bishop and Co.)
· Houndsditch

J. Murray
· 54 Great Queen St

1888

C. Clark
· 53 Temple St, Manchester

1890

Andrews and Co.
(*Champion Parlour Dramas*)
· St Luke's

c1890

Goode Bros
(*The King's Theatre*)
· Clerkenwell Green, Clerkenwell Rd

Yates and Co.
(*The Penny Theatre Royal*)
· Old Radford Works, Nottingham

c1900

The Globe Drama
· Colour-printed in Germany

BOYS' MAGAZINES WHICH PUBLISHED TOY THEATRES

Of these, *Boys of England* was by far the most successful.

1865

Temple Publishing Co.
· *Black Eyed Susan*

1866-80

Charles Stevens succeeded by:
Edwin J. Brett
· *Boys of England*

c1870

Charles Fox
· *The Boy's Standard*

Henderson
· *Jack Harkaway*

Hogarth House
· *Tyburn Dick*

c1880-90

Arthur Bailey
· *The Boy's Halfpenny Budget*

ARTISTIC REVIVALS

1901-1904

Elkin Mathews
Vigo St
Jack B. Yeats

1922-23

Wells, Gardner & Darton Ltd
(drawn by Albert Rutherson)
· F. J. Harvey Darton

GERMANY

c1820

Arnz and Co
· Dusseldorf

Carl Kühn
· Berlin

Johann Raab
· Nuremberg

C Schauer
· Berlin

c1825

J. M. Hermann
· Munich

c1830

G.P.Buchner
· Nuremberg

Joseph Scholz
· Mainz

L.Steffan
· Berlin

Winckelmann and Söhne
· Berlin

c1835

Gustav Kühn
· Neuruppin

c1840

F.N.Campe
· Nuremberg

F.Guillaume
· Berlin

C.Hellriegel
· Berlin

Oehmigke and Riemschneider
· Neuruppin

G.N.Renner and Co.
· Nuremberg

F.G.Schulz
· Stuttgart

c1845

Hermann and Barth
· Munich

c1850

Aleiter and Zeitinger
· Mainz

F.Fechter
· Guben

Halder and Cronberger
· Stuttgart

G.Löwensohn
· Furth Bei Nuremberg

J.F.Richter
· Hamburg

Scmitt Bros
· Nuremberg

c1855

J.C.Renner
· Nuremberg

C.Schramm
· Nuremberg

c1860

F.W.Bergemann
· Neuruppin

Braun and Schneider
· Munich

E.D.Büttner and Co.
· Berlin

J.C.Hochwind
· Munich

Linn and Co.
· Mainz

J.Ringler
· Augsburg

E.D.Stange
· Berlin

c1870

E.Roth
· Stuttgart

Schaal and Wagner
· Stuttgart

c1877

J.F.Schreiber
· Esslingen

c1880

Adolf Engel
· Berlin

Robrahn and Co.
· Magdeburg

c1890

John and Moser
· Magdeburg

Schmidt and Romer
· Leipzig

DENMARK

from 1850

E.O.Jordan
· Copenhagen

c1860

T.H.Mathiesen
· Copenhagen

c1865

Michaelsen and Tilge
· Copenhagen

1880-1924

Alfred Jacobsen
· Copenhagen

1914-35

Carl Aller's *Illustrated Family Journal*
· Copenhagen

1930

Vilhelm Prior's bookshop
· Copenhagen

1936-64

Prior's bookshop
(Anne and Estrid Prior)
· Copenhagen

1941-49

Carl Aller's *Pegasus Theatre*
· Copenhagen

1945

Carl Larsen
· Copenhagen

1964-76

Prior's Dukketeater (Estrid Prior)
· Copenhagen

1976-85

Prior's Dukketeater (Egon Petersen)
· Copenhagen

1985-

Prior's Dukketeater (Hanne Nelander)
· Copenhagen

FRANCE

1820-

Imagerie Pellerin
· Epinal

c1833

F. C. Wentzel
· Weissembourg, Paris

c1850

Didion
· Metz

c1860

C. Burkardt
· Weissembourg

Gangel
· Metz

c1861-88

O. Pinot
· Epinal

c1870

Imagerie Réunies
· Jarville, Nancy

La Poupée Modèle
· Paris

c1890

Dehalt
· Nancy

1904-1905

Albert Mericand (*Mon Théâtre*)
· Paris

AUSTRIA

c1820

J. and M. Trentsensky
· Vienna

c1870

Stockinger and Morsak
· Vienna

c1885

G. Levy
· Vienna

F. Paterno
· Vienna

c1890

G. Freytag and Berndt
· Vienna

1950

J. Schneider Jun.
· Vienna

SPAIN

c1900

Estampa Economica Paluzie
· Barcelona

c1925

Seix and Barral
· Barcelona

ITALY

c1880

O. Bianchi
· Milan

A. Borigione
· Milan

Lebrun, Boldetti
· Milan

c1890

Cromo Lit. Arte
· Milan

c1900

A. Giore
· Milan

c1920

Carroccio
· Milan

AMERICA

c1870

Scott and Co.
(Seltz's *American Boys' Theatre*)
· 146 Fulton St, New York

c1888-89

Richard Schwarz
· New York

c1900

McLoughlin Bros
· New York

J. H. Singer
· 31st St, New York

PAPERS AND MAGAZINES PUBLISHING
TOY THEATRES

1896

Baltimore Sunday Herald
· Baltimore

Boston Sunday Globe
· Boston

1918

Delineator Magazine
· Butterick Building, New York

1933

Child Life Magazine
· Rand McNally Building, Chicago

Bibliography

Arthur B. Allen, *The Model Theatre* (London, 1950)

Alan J. Allport, *Model Theatres and How to Make Them* (London, 1978)

H.C. Andrews, 'A Note on H.G. Clarke's productions', *Notes and Queries* (London, 6 May 1944)

Isabelle Anscombe, 'Cut out a piece of Pure Melodrama', *The Times* (4 May 1985)

Theo Arthur, 'The Toy Theatre', *The Era Almanack* (London, 1891)

John Ashton, 'Childhood's Drama', in *Varia* (London, 1894)

Cyril Beaumont, 'A Votary of Thespis', in *Flashback* (London, 1931)

G.W. Bishop, 'The Toy Theatre, A Penny Plain Twopence Coloured – A talk with Mr Pollock', article in *The Times* (London, 21 December 1930)

F.B. Brady, 'Juvenile Drama', review in *Theatre Notebook* (London, 1946)

Eric Brammall, 'A Toy Theatre Centenary', *Drama* (Winter 1956)

G.K. Chesterton, 'The Toy Theatre', in *Tremendous Trifles* (London, 1909)
– *Autobiography* (London, 1936)

Peter Davidson and Alan Powers, *Grantchester Revisited and Greatly Improved – A Masque for Toy Theatre* (Cambridge, 1977)

A.C.E., letter, *Notes and Queries* (London, 23 May 1931), p 377
– letter, *Notes and Queries* (London, 27 June 1931)

Max Eickemeyer, *Das Kindertheater* (Esslingen, 1900)

Hugo Elm, *Das Kindertheater* (Esslingen, 1886)

Kenneth Fawdry (ed), *Toy Theatre* (London, 1980)

Politikens Forlag (pub), *Vi Spiller Dukketeater* (Copenhagen, 1969)

H.E. Frances-Eagle, *The Glamour of a Toy Shop* (London, 1913)
– 'The Webb Juvenile Drama', *The Mask*, V (Florence, 1912-13), pp 347-52

George Garde, *Theater Geschichte Im Spiegel Der Kindertheater* ('The Theatre as reflected in the Toy Theatre') (Copenhagen, 1971)

Edward Gordon Craig (alias Allen Carric), '"Captain Jack B. Yeats". A Pirate of the Old School', *The Mask*, V (Florence, 1912-13)

– (alias Edward Edwardovitch), 'The Best Theatre in London', *The Mask*, V (Florence, 1912-13)
– (alias Dorothy Nevile Lees), 'Robert Louis Stevenson and the Drama of Skelt', *The Mask*, V (Florence, 1912-13)

Walter Hamilton, 'Skelt and Webb', *Notes and Queries* (London, 1 November 1890), p 344

Hugh Harting, 'The Mantle of Skelt', *Notes and Queries* (London, January 1931), p 171
– letter from *Johannesburg Sunday Times*, *Notes and Queries* (London, April 1931), p 253

Kerstin Holmberg, *Modellteater Boken* (Vallentuna, 1986)

Langley Levi, letter from *Johannesburg Sunday Times*, *Notes and Queries* (London, June 1931), p 409

Alfred Lunt, 'Alfred Lunt presents Penny Plain and Twopence Coloured', *Theatre Arts* (New York, January 1947)

Paul McPharlin, *The Puppet Theatre in America*, 2nd edn (Boston, 1969)

Gerald Morice, letter re the last days of B. Pollock's shop, *Notes and Queries* (London, October 1943)

John Oxenford, 'The Toy Theatre', *The Era Almanack* (London, 1871)

Kurt Pfluger and Helmut Herbst, *Schreiber's Kinder Theater* (Pinneberg, 1986)

Walter Röhler, 'Towards a History of Paper Theatre', *Puppetry USA* (Birmingham, MI, 1937)
– 'The German Toy Theatre', *Theatre* (Bradford Civic Playhouse, Winter 1948)
– *Grosse Liebe Zu Kleinen Theatern* (Hamburg, 1963)

Inge Sauer, *Theater Aus Papier* (Cologne, 1989)

Norman H. Schneider, *The Model Vaudeville Theatre* (New York, 1909)

Desmond Seaton-Reid, 'An Early West Sheet', *Theatre Notebook*, IV (London, 1949)
– 'Early West Plates', *Theatre Notebook*, V (London, 1950)
– 'A Portrait of William West', *Theatre Notebook*, VI (London, 1951)

Roy Smith, *Three Model Theatres* (Edinburgh, 1960)

George Speaight, *Juvenile Drama. The history of the English Toy Theatre* (London, 1946), 2nd edn published as *Toy Theatre* (London, 1969)
– 'Pope in the Toy Theatre', *Theatre Notebook*, VII (London, 1952-53), pp 62-3
– 'The M.W. Stone Collection', *Theatre Notebook*, XI (London, 1956-57), p 62-3
– 'Juvenile Drama and Puppetry Research', *Theatre Notebook*, XXI (London, 1967-68), pp 24-6
– 'The Brigand of the Toy Theatre', in *The Saturday Book*, 29 (London, 1969)
– 'The Toy Theatre', *Harvard Library Bulletin*, no 19, (Harvard, 1971), pp 307-13

– 'Was there ever an American Toy Theatre', in *Nineteenth Century Theatre Research*, I (1973), pp 89-93

– 'The Toy Theatre in England', *V & A Theatre Museum Card*, no 16 (HMSO, 1977)

– 'The Toy Theatre in Europe', *V & A Theatre Museum Card*, no 17 (HMSO, 1977)

– A union catalogue for the Juvenile Drama of seven major collections (in preparation, London)

H. D. Spencer, 'A West Artist', *Theatre Notebook*, IV (London, 1949), pp 37-8

– 'Juvenile Drama's Artist – William Heath's Early Sheets', *Theatre Notebook*, V (London, 1950), pp 43-4

Robert Louis Stevenson, 'A Penny Plain and Twopence Coloured', *Magazine of Art* (London, 1884), reprinted in *Memories and Portraits* (London, 1887), Chatto & Windus edn (London, 1920)

M. W. Stone, *The Juvenile Drama* (unpublished manuscript, 1944)

– 'Juvenile Drama and J. H. Jameson', *Theatre Notebook*, I (London, 1945-46), pp 5-6

– 'Unrecorded Plays Published by William West', *Theatre Notebook*, I (London, 1945-46), pp 33-4

– 'William Blake and the Juvenile Drama', *Theatre Notebook*, I (London, 1945-46), p 41

– 'Juvenile Drama Publishers – The Dyers', *Theatre Notebook*, I (London, 1945-46), p 80

– 'Jonathan King's Juvenile Drama Collection', *Theatre Notebook*, II (London, 1946-48), p 57

– 'Shakespeare and the Juvenile Drama', *Theatre Notebook*, VIII (London, 1953-54), pp 65-6

Povl Syskind and Paul Brandt, *Alfred Jacobsens Teaterdekorationer og Danske Billeder* ('Alfred Jacobsen's Theatre Sets and Danish Pictures') (Dansk Dukketeaterforening, Copenhagen, 1967)

Ralph Thomas, 'West's Toy Theatre Prints', *Notes and Queries* (London, December 1873), p 463

– 'The Skelt's', *Notes and Queries* (London, 27 August 1898), p 161

– 'G. Cruickshank and G. Childs', *Notes and Queries* (London, 11 March 1916), p 203

– 'The Cruickshanks, Artists and West and Jameson, Publishers', *Notes and Queries* (London, 9 October 1920), pp 281-5

Joseph Viscomi, *Playing with Toy Theatre (An essay on the toy and the theatre it illustrates)* (New York, 1977)

Thomas Walton, 'Notes for a History of Juvenile Drama', *Theatre Notebook*, III (London, 1948-49), pp 64-6

– 'A French Toy Theatre', *Theatre* (Bradford Civic Playhouse, Winter 1947)

– 'French Toy Theatre Again', *Theatre* (Bradford Civic Playhouse, Autumn 1948)

Maisie Ward, *Gilbert Keith Chesterton* (London, 1944)

H. J. Webb, letter, *Notes and Queries* (London, June 1931), p 409

Wells, Gardner, Darton and Co. Limited (eds), *Chatterbox* (London, 1923)

H. W. Whanslaw, 'The Toy That Never Grows Old', in *Chatterbox* (London, 1923), reprinted as *Everybody's Theatre* (London, 1926)

– The Bankside Stage Book (London, no date)

Charles D. Williams, 'A note on A. N. Myers and Co.', *Notes and Queries* (London, 29 January 1944)

– 'A note on H. G. Clarke's Productions', *Notes and Queries* (London, 22 April 1944)

– 'A note on the "Globe" Drama', *Notes and Queries* (London, 3 June 1944)

Guy R. Williams, *Making a Miniature Theatre* (London, 1967)

A. E. Wilson, *Penny Plain, Twopence Coloured* (London, 1932)

Peter Winn, *Plays by British publishers represented in the Sage Collection* (unpublished dissertation, University of Victoria, British Columbia, 1975)

Jack Yeats, 'How Jack B. Yeats produced his plays for the Miniature Stage', *The Mask*, V (Florence, 1912-13)

Herbert Zwiauer, *Papier Theater (Bühnenwelt en Miniature)* (Vienna, 1987)

EXHIBITION CATALOGUES

Arquetecturas di Papel, exh cat, Madrid, 1980

Das Papier Theater im 19. Jahrhundert, exh cat, Bundesrealgymnasiums Reutte im Tiroler Landestheater, no date

Papier Theater, exh cat, Puppentheatersammlung, Stadt Museum, Munich, 1977

Papier Theater, exh cat, Osterreichische Museum Fur Volkskunde, Vienna, 1985

Theaterzauber Aus Papier, exh cat, Theater An Der Wilhelmhohe, Lingen, 9-30 April 1978

The Toy Theatre, exh cat, Camden Arts Centre, London, 14 December 1977 – 8 January 1978

NEWSPAPER CUTTINGS

Interview with Louisa Pollock, *Evening Standard* (1 September 1938)

'Obituary of Benjamin Pollock', *The Times* (7 August 1937)

'Obituary of H. J. Webb', *Daily Mail* (29 December 1933)

'The Toy Theatre (The Old Shop Carries On)', *Observer* (27 November 1938)

'Toy Theatres Saved', *Sunday Times* (23 January 1944)

'U. S. Museums Collect Toy Pantomimes', *Observer* (16 January 1944)

Public collections of toy theatres and prints

Toronto:

University of Toronto (Rare Book Department)
Desmond Seaton-Reid Collection

DENMARK

Copenhagen:

Prior's Dukketeater, Copenhagen
An international collection of stages and models permanently on display in Prior's Bookshop

GERMANY

Darmstadt:

Walter Röhler Collection
At the time of writing, this collection was in the process of being transferred from the Deutsches Institut Fur Puppenspiel, Bochum.

Hanau:

Papiertheater Museum

Munich:

Stadt Museum
A comprehensive collection of toy theatre material is in the Puppet Theatre Collection.

GREAT BRITAIN

Derby:

The Derby Museum
Frank Bradley Collection of toy theatres and prints
Anthony Denning Collection of Trentsensky sheets

London:

British Museum (Print Room)
The Ralph Thomas Collection of early English publishers
Museum of London
The Jonathan King Collection of tinsel pictures and prints
Pollock's Toy Museum
English, European and American model stages, together with a comprehensive private collection of prints
Victoria and Albert Museum (Theatre Museum)
The M. W. Stone Collection
The Herbert Hinkins Collection

Oxford:

Christchurch College Library
F. B. Brady Collection of toy theatre material

UNITED STATES

Harvard:

Harvard College Library
The Harvard Theatre Collection contains an international collection of toy theatre prints

New York City:

Columbia University
Brander Matthews Dramatic Museum Collection of stages and prints
Museum of the City of New York
The Alfred Lunt Collection of toy theatres
New York Public Library
Library and Museum of the Performing Arts
The Hiram Stead Collection

Santa Fe:

Museum of New Mexico
Museum of International Folk Art Girard Foundation Collection. This contains an international collection of toy theatre prints with particular emphasis on the English Juvenile Drama.

Photographic acknowledgements

Grateful acknowledgement is due to the following for supplying photographic material and for permission to reproduce it.

Author's Collection Fig 2, 4, 5, 6, 8, 9, 11, 13, 14, 15, 16, 17, 20, 21, 23, 24, 25, 26, 29, 30, 31, 32, 33, 34, 35, 36, 37, 38, 39, 40, 41, 42, 43, 46, 47, 48, 49, 50, 53, 54, 55, 57, 58, 67, 68, 69, 70, 71, 73, 74, 75, 76, 77, 78, 79, 81, 82, 83, 84, 85, 86, 89, 90, 94, 95, 96, 97, 98, 99, 100, 104, 107, 109, 110, 111, 112, 113, 116, 117;

(photographs Richard Goulding) Pl I, II, III, IV, V, VI, VII, VIII, IX, X, XI, XII, XIII, XIV, XV, XVI, XVII, XVIII, XIX, XX, XXI, XXII, XXIII, XXIV, XXV, XXVI, XXVII, XXVIII, XXIX, XXX, XXXI, XXXII;

(photographs Walter Röhler) Fig 51, 52

British Museum (courtesy of the Trustees) Fig 7, 12

Derby Museum Fig 18, 22, 45, 59, 92, 93

Harvard College Library Theatre Collection Fig 3

Illustrated London News Picture Library Fig 28

Imagerie Pellerin d'Epinal Fig 115

Denys Ingram Publishers Fig 44

Alan Keen (courtesy of family) Fig 27

Serge Lifar Collection (photograph Sotheby's) Fig 102, 105

Hildegarde Metzsch (photographs Ulrich Dagge) Fig 56, 65, 66, 72, 80

Museum of London Fig 10

National Museum, Copenhagen Fig 61, 62

Prior's Dukketeater (courtesy of Hanne Nelander) Frontispiece; Fig 60, 63, 64, 114

From the collections of the **Theatre Museum** (reproduced by courtesy of the Trustees of the Victoria and Albert Museum) Fig 19, 101, 103, 106, 108

John Vickers Theatre Collection Fig 1

Ab Vissers Collection, Holland Fig 87, 88

Christopher Williams Collection Fig 91

Every effort has been made to contact copyright-holders of photographs. Any copyright-holders who have not been reached or to whom inaccurate acknowledgement has been made are invited to contact the publishers.

Index